Slow Looking

Slow Looking

The Art and Practice of Learning Through Observation

Shari Tishman

Routledge
Taylor & Francis Group

NEW YORK AND LONDON

First published 2018
by Routledge
711 Third Avenue, New York, NY 10017

and by Routledge
2 Park Square, Milton Park, Abingdon, Oxon, OX14 4RN

Routledge is an imprint of the Taylor & Francis Group, an informa business

© 2018 Taylor & Francis

Library of Congress Cataloging-in-Publication Data
Names: Tishman, Shari, author.
Title: Slow looking : the art and practice of learning through observation / Shari Tishman.
Description: New York, NY ; Abingdon, Oxon : Routledge, 2018. | Includes bibliographical references and index.
Identifiers: LCCN 2017023985 (print) | LCCN 2017044953 (ebook) | ISBN 9781315283814 (e-book) | ISBN 9781138240407 (hardback) | ISBN 9781138240414 (pbk) | ISBN 9781315283814 (ebk)
Subjects: LCSH: Observation (Educational method) | Critical thinking—Study and teaching—Methodology.
Classification: LCC LB1027.28 (ebook) | LCC LB1027.28 .T57 2018 (print) | DDC 371.3/8—dc23
LC record available at https://lccn.loc.gov/2017023985

ISBN: 978-1-138-24040-7 (hbk)
ISBN: 978-1-138-24041-4 (pbk)
ISBN: 978-1-315-28381-4 (ebk)

Typeset in Bembo
by Florence Production Ltd, Stoodleigh, Devon

For Martin Andic

We only see what we look at. To look is an act of choice.

—John Berger

Go to Nature; take the facts into your own hands; look, and see for yourself!

—Louis Aggasiz

To see takes time—like to have a friend takes time.

—Georgia O'Keefe

Contents

Acknowledgements

This book has been a while in the making. I have the good fortune of working at Project Zero, a research center at the Harvard Graduate School of Education (HGSE), and it is hard to imagine a more supportive and stimulating community of colleagues. I am grateful to all of my friends at Project Zero for their ongoing inspiration and encouragement. I am also indebted to the many school teachers and museum educators connected to Project Zero over the years who have allowed me to learn from their experiences.

I owe a special thanks to David Perkins. Many of the ideas in this book were tested, explored, and made better through our countless good conversations. I am exceptionally grateful to Edward Clapp and Liz Dawes Duraisingh, who helped me develop a concrete vision of this book and coached me through the early stages of making it a reality. I warmly thank my friend and Project Zero colleague Carrie James for her steady, day-to-day encouragement, and for always being ready with a practical suggestion and an inspirational idea.

I am grateful to the many friends and colleagues who have conversed with me about ideas that found their way into the book: I appreciate the walk-and-talks with Patty Stone, and the tea-and-talks with Alythea McKinney. A special thanks to Seymour Simmons for helping me explore the connections between slow looking and drawing, and to Corinne Zimmerman for our many stimulating conversations about slow looking in museums. I thank Scott Reuscher for always directing me to the right poet, and I am deeply grateful to Jordy Oakland for her help with some early literary research that got me started. I am indebted to Jessica Ross for her insightful help in applying "slow", to classroom practice, and I thank Jim Reese for allowing me to work some of these ideas out on stage, sometimes before they were ready for prime time. I am grateful to Howard Gardner for his kind encouragement.

Some of the ideas in the book connected to the Out of Eden Learn project were developed under a grant from the Abundance Foundation. I gratefully acknowledge the foundation's support, and I am particularly appreciative of the support and counsel of its president, Stephen Kahn. A special thanks to Paul Salopek, the original Out of Eden walker, whose work and friendship have provided inspiration along the way. I warmly thank Susie Blair for partnering with me on analyzing the student data from Out of Eden Learn, and I thank Michelle Nguyen for her invaluable help during the later stages of that work.

Throughout this book, various works of art are referenced in the text or reprinted at a small scale in black and white. I am grateful to the artists, museums, and scholars who have allowed me to reprint their work, and I encourage readers to supplement their reading experience by searching for full-color versions of these works online.

Dan Schwartz, my editor at Routledge, has provided welcome encouragement and valuable feedback. I am profoundly grateful to Allison Wigen, who assisted in the development of the manuscript and provided wisdom, encouragement and practical assistance at precisely the moments they were needed. My sister, Andrea Tishman, has truly been along on this journey since the beginning: So much is due to her ready ear, constant encouragement, and insightful eye. I thank my husband Robert Sowa and my son Stefan Sowa for their loving support every step of the way.

This book is dedicated to the memory of Martin Andic—professor, friend, and a true teacher of "slow," whose inspiration so many years ago started me along the path.

CHAPTER 1

Introduction: Slow Matters

In Oakland, California, four ninth graders wielding screwdrivers sit around a table and take apart a doorknob. Using their hands and their eyes, they explore the doorknob's intricacies and interconnected parts. On the table in front of them is a large sheet of paper on which they make notes and sketches, documenting their discoveries as they go along.

In Central Asia, a journalist is traveling by foot along the route of the ancient Silk Road. A practitioner of slow journalism, he is listening for stories that don't make headline news. In a suburb outside of Samarkand, Uzbekistan, he stops to visit with a traditional papermaker. He watches a waterwheel power wooden mallets that pound tree bark into a fibrous pulp. He writes that when the paper is dried and polished, it feels as soft as silk.

At the Museum of Fine Arts in Boston, Massachusetts, a group of medical residents gathers in front of a large painting. Their purpose is to develop their observation skills through looking at art. A museum guide tells them to look closely at the painting and talk about what they see. As the conversation unfolds, the residents are surprised to discover how differently they each interpret the painting, even though they are all drawing on the same visual clues. The experience causes them to think anew about their own clinical practices.

Across the river in Cambridge, Massachusetts, middle school student bends close to a computer screen and enters the immersive virtual environment of a pond ecosystem. Shrinking herself down so she can get into a micro-submarine, she explores the pond floor where she discovers some microscopic organisms. She carefully observes their behavior over a period of virtual days.

In Chennai, India, an 11-year-old girl takes a slow walk through her neighborhood with the intention of looking at her familiar environment with fresh eyes. She takes pictures and makes notes of things she has never noticed before. Later, she logs into an online forum where she posts the story of her walk. While she's there, she browses the posts of students in other countries who have taken similar walks and looks at their neighborhoods through their eyes.

These are stories of slow looking in action. The definition of slow looking is straightforward. It simply means taking the time to carefully observe more than meets the eye at first glance. It is happening in each of these vignettes, and it happens anywhere people take a generous amount of time to observe the world closely—in classrooms, in art galleries, in laboratories, online, in backyard gardens, and on neighborhood walks.

This book is an exploration of slow looking as a mode of learning. The term slow looking uses the vernacular of the visual, but it is important to emphasize that learning through prolonged observation can occur through all of the senses. Most of the examples and ideas in this book are about visual observation, but many aren't, and I often use the term "look" to refer to sensory observation more broadly. So, for example, I might say that the ninth-graders in the opening vignette are "looking" at a doorknob with their hands as well as their eyes.

Whatever sensory form that it takes, slow looking is a way of gaining knowledge about the world. It helps us discern complexities that can't be grasped quickly, and it involves a distinctive set of skills and dispositions that have a different center of gravity than those involved in other modes of learning. I believe that it is also a learnable practice.

I came to the topic of slow looking in a roundabout way. I work as an educational researcher, and my focus is on what people in my field sometimes call high-level cognition. I'm interested in forms of thinking that go beyond basic literacies, and my research projects often focus on programs and practices that help people learn to think critically, reflectively, and creatively.

For many years, learning through observation wasn't something I thought about a great deal. If I thought about observation at all, it was as a means to an end—something one did to gather data, which would then feed into higher-level thinking processes like reasoning or problem solving. But eventually I started to see things differently. I remember the first time my new awareness began to crystallize. I was visiting a fifth-grade class-room, and it was the beginning of the school day. Students were noisily spilling into class, and the teacher told me she was planning to spend the next half hour having them look at a painting by Matisse. I nodded politely. What I was really thinking was this: Tell a group of fifth-graders to sit still and look at a painting for 30 minutes, and you will very quickly have a classroom of squirming, restless kids. But the teacher had a plan. She used some simple strategies to help students prolong their observations beyond a first glance, and it was amazing how effective they were. These were *really* simple strategies, like asking students to make a list of five things they notice and then going around in a circle and having each student make an observation that expands on something someone previously said. And having students turn to someone else and share two questions they had. Half an hour flew by.

At each fresh round of observations, the teacher gave students plenty of time to look. What she didn't do was give them much textbook infor-mation about the painting. Nonetheless, it was stunning how much students learned. For example, as their observations accumulated, they began to discern the structural complexity of the work—the way the various forms and colors and lines worked together to form a whole. They also detected several ambiguities in the painting—aspects of it that could be interpreted in different ways. The painting was of a colorful, vividly patterned dining room, with an empty chair next to a table. The students wondered who the chair was for. The artist, maybe? They even envisioned themselves sitting in the chair and imagined what it would feel like. (Nice, they thought, but maybe a little claustrophobic.) And so on. Even if the students didn't come to consensus about the "correct" interpretation of the painting (if indeed there is one), and even though they couldn't recite historical information about the work, they had clearly learned a great deal. Moreover, the knowledge they gained depended wholly on the fact that they were looking long and closely for themselves. No amount of outside information could have replaced the insights they gained.

After this experience, I started noticing the power of slow looking in other settings as well—inside and outside of schools. I became fascinated by how intrinsically engaging slow looking could be with just a little bit of structure to sustain it. I came to see it as a form of active cognition with an intrinsically rewarding feedback loop: the more you look, the more you see; the more you see, the more engaged you become. I began to wonder about the commonalities in observational practices across different contexts—in the arts and humanities, in science, and in everyday life. I sought out research projects where I could learn more about slow looking, and I increasingly incorporated slow looking into my own university teaching. I became interested in the presence of slow looking in historical ideas about schooling, and in the history of museums. I grew curious about the connection between slow looking and the history of scientific observation, and about the connection between slow looking and literary description. Throughout, I continued to try to understand the learning benefits of slow looking and the educational practices that supported them.

This book is the story of where these inquiries led. I've written it with educators in mind, and if you are looking for practical ideas and strategies to use in the classroom, you will find several of them here, particularly in the earlier and final chapters. You'll also find some exercises that invite you to try slow looking yourself. But many of the ideas and examples discussed in the book go far beyond the classroom. My hope is that the book will be of interest to anyone who is curious about slow looking— what it is, how to do it, and why it matters.

Slow is in the air

I am definitely not alone in my interest. An appreciation of all things slow is part of the culture these days, and there seems to be a date when it started. In 1986, an Italian food and wine journalist named Carlos Petrini organized a demonstration on the Spanish Steps in Rome in order to protest the intended opening of a MacDonald's restaurant on the site. The event was credited with sparking the slow food movement, which celebrates local foods, sustainable food production, and the slow enjoyment of the traditional pleasures of the table. The movement has since spread worldwide, and continues to thrive today. It is part of what seems to be a growing appetite for "slow" in contemporary culture. To give just a few examples: There is "slow art day"—an annual event held in museums around the world, with very simple rules: go to an art museum, look at five pieces for 5 to 10 minutes each; then have lunch with someone and talk about what you saw. There is also a slow education movement that eschews a fast-food model of schooling designed to deliver what it calls "packages of test-shaped knowledge" and instead argues for schooling that encourages in-depth learning and quality interactions between teachers and students.[1] And there's "slow journalism," practiced by a growing number of journalists who refuse to feed the public craving for instant information and instead emphasize moving slowly through the world, listening carefully to its stories, and reporting at a human pace.

Not all of these slow trends foreground slow *looking*, but they all involve moving beyond first impressions toward more immersive, prolonged experiences that unfold slowly over time. To some extent, this book is part of that trend. But there are some features of slow looking as I define it that may not fit with the larger trend. One is that I don't believe slow looking is necessarily characterized by a quiet, meditative mood. As I learned when I walked into that fifth-grade classroom, prolonged observation can be an energetic, lively affair. Of course, it can also be peaceful and tranquil, and, even spiritual for some. But it needn't be any of these things. I come back to this point in a later chapter, but I mention it now because I want to be clear that I lean toward an expansive rather than narrow view of slow looking; people of almost all ages can do it, and it can happen in many moods and at many tempos.

Nor do I believe that slow looking is necessarily anti-technology, even though the speed of digital life can pose a challenge to "slow". We live in the digital age. Immersive social media, omnipresent news streams, endless information at the tap of a finger—all have the potential to fracture attention spans. But digital technologies and media can also be powerful tools to help people look closely at things they may otherwise overlook. For example, thanks to NASA's social media presence, at this writing millions of people recently spent quite a bit of time looking at pictures of rocky, barren comets as they hurtle through space. Through digital crowd sourcing, thousands of people now aid scientists in their careful observations of the natural world. Through media images gone viral, hundreds of thousands of people carefully scrutinize the actions of public figures. Our fast-paced, digitized culture may present challenges to slow looking, but it also offers opportunities.

There are three main reasons why it is important to pay attention to slow looking. These reasons may feel especially pressing in the digital age, but they are not unique to it.

1. Slow looking is an important counterbalance to the natural human tendency toward fast looking. Most of the time, we scan our visual environments rapidly, unreflectively taking in whatever surface information is readily available and briskly moving on. We make first impressions quickly, and they tend to stick. Moreover, when we're in this fast mode we tend toward fill-in-the-blank looking. A few well-placed brush strokes and we "see" a whole face, just as we get the gist of a song by hearing just a few lines. Usually fast looking serves us pretty well. It would be absurdly inconvenient to have to look at things over and over again in order to recognize them. Intuitive, visual sense-making is necessary in order to move through the world efficiently. But some things take more than a quick glance to fully apprehend. When you look at a map of an unfamiliar city you can see quickly that it's a map, but you'll need to study it for a while in order to make use of the information it offers. You can often get the gist of things by looking at them fairly quickly, but uncovering their complexity takes time. A brief glance at a tree tells you that it has a trunk, branches, and leaves. But it takes time to notice the variegated pattern of lichen on its bark, the irregular shape of its canopy, and the myriad creatures that are part of its ecosystem.

2. *Slow looking tends to be under-emphasized in general education.* The mind's most productive work doesn't always come naturally. Shifting gears from fast looking to slow looking parallels how cognitive psychologists talk about the fast mind and the slow mind.[2] The fast mind is characterized by rapid, intuitive, automatic judgments—including judgments made through visual first impressions—and it is the mind's most prevalent operating mode. The slow mind is characterized by deliberative, careful thought. Its hallmarks are reasoning with evidence, analytical thinking, and careful decision making. The rewards of slow thinking are huge (consider the entire projects of modern science and Western philosophy), but slowing the mind down and getting it to forego fast intuitive judgment in favor of slow deliberation takes vigilance, willpower, and training.

In educational circles, most people agree on the value of training the deliberative mind. Educators (including me) espouse the importance of teaching young people to reason with evidence, to analyze and evaluate arguments skillfully, and to make judgments thoughtfully. We regard these capacities as general thinking skills that are useful in all subject matters and in everyday life. Many school curricula purport to teach these essential skills, and developing the capacity to think critically is part of what people often mean when they describe a good general education.

The teaching of slow looking, on the other hand, tends to be a more specialized affair. A high school student might get a chance to practice slow looking in an art history class or a science lab. But developing the capacity to observe the world slowly isn't usually put forth as a core educational goal. This is unfortunate, because slow looking has the same wide applicability as slow thinking, but the skill sets are somewhat different. Slow thinking involves analyzing information, weighing evidence, and making careful inferences. Slow looking, on the other hand, foregrounds the capacity to observe details, to defer interpretation, to make careful discernments, to shift between different perspectives, to be aware of subjectivity, and to purposefully use a variety of observation strategies in order to move past first impressions. There is overlap, of course. For example, both slow thinking and slow looking emphasize the capacity to look at things from different perspectives and to seek information from a variety of sources. But neither area subsumes the other, and giving educational attention to one area won't fully develop capacities in the other.

3. *Looking closely is a shared human value.* People disagree about many things, but few people disagree about the value of careful observation. Most of us intuitively understand that the world is a complex place, and that we often rush to judgments about how to resolve or untangle its complexities a bit too quickly. Slow looking is a healthy response to complexity because it creates a space for the multiple dimensions of things to be perceived and appreciated. But it is a response that, while rooted in natural instinct, requires intention to sustain. This is easier said than done. Often, the most important moments to slow down and look carefully are also the hardest: political disagreement, personal disputes, conflicting values—all have to do with clashing beliefs about how things are or should be. But conflict is often a symptom of complexity—a sign that there is more to things than meets the eye. Imagine an education that trained us to recognize conflict as a cue to examine complexity rather than a cue to dismiss it.

A key argument of this book is that slow looking is, to a large extent, a *learned* capacity. The problem isn't so much that people don't believe in its importance; it's that they haven't been helped to develop the skills and dispositions to support it. Contemporary Western education emphasizes the role of rational, critical thought in the pursuit of knowledge. Slow looking may not typically be identified as a core educational value, but its contribution to critical thinking is foundational: before we can decide what is true and right, it's important to simply look closely at what's at hand.

Notes

1   See, for example, http://www.slowmovement.com/slow_schools.php.
2   For the most comprehensive review of this work, see Kahneman, D. (2011). *Thinking, Fast and Slow*. New York: Farrar, Strauss and Giroux.

CHAPTER 2

Strategies for Looking

Slow looking is everywhere. It is part of the daily work of experts, in the way that systematic scientific observation is part of the study of biology, and it is a common practice in everyday life—something we do when we take time to carefully examine a painting in a museum or a family photograph or an insect on the sidewalk. The practice of slow looking isn't an esoteric pursuit, but it is often a strategic one because it involves the intentional use of observation strategies to guide and focus the eye. If you've ever used a checklist to observe birds in your backyard, set a schedule to systematically notice changes in a garden over time, or intentionally softened your gaze to see a painting in a new light, you've used an observation strategy, which works by providing the eye with various kinds of structures and expectations.

Specialists in different areas look closely at very different kinds of things. Forensic anthropologists scrutinize skeletons. Mariners observe patterns of winds and waves. Psychologists observe patterns of human behavior. Educators look closely for signs of student learning. Though the things they look at may vary, the basic strategies that experts use to make observations are strikingly similar across disciplines. Moreover, the strategies themselves are quite simple: anyone can learn how to use them, and they can be seen at work in all sorts of human endeavors. This chapter looks at four of these broad observation strategies, drawing examples from science, art, and everyday life.

Categories to Guide the Eye

It's a rainy Saturday afternoon, and the entrance hall of the art museum echoes with chatter as visitors shake out umbrellas and line up to purchase tickets. In a corner of the hall a group of people gather under a sign.

Public tour begins here at 2:00 PM

Slow Looking

All Welcome

Soon, a museum guide arrives. She introduces herself to the group, exchanges a few pleasantries, then leads the visitors down a hall and into a large, high-ceilinged gallery filled with nineteenth-century American paintings. She pauses to give people a moment to soak in the space, and then gathers them around a large painting of a seascape.

The visitors look at the painting for a moment, then peer at the wall placard next to it. Then they look back to the guide expectantly, waiting to hear what she has to say. Instead of launching into a lecture, the guide says, "Let's start by just looking at the painting and noticing its features. I have three questions for you: What colors do you see? What shapes do you see? What lines do you see? Let's start with colors."

Try This

Color, Shape, Line

Use this strategy with an art image, a view of nature, a cityscape, or whatever environment you happen to be in now.

What colors do you see?

Describe several.

What shapes do you see?

Describe several.

What lines do you see?

Describe several.

Do it alone, or do it with someone else and share your observations.

The group is quiet for a moment, and then someone speaks.

"I see a gray sky."

"I see white clouds, streaked with gray and violet," someone else says.

"There's a pale yellow glow in the upper right corner of the painting," another visitor chimes in. "It looks like the sun is trying to come through."

Soon, everyone is pointing out colors in the sky. Eventually, people's attention shifts downward to the lower half of the painting and they start describing the color of the sea. At first they describe it as blue or bluish-green. But someone points out a streak of silvery purple, and suddenly the visitors begin to see a variety of hues and tones in the water that they hadn't seen at first. Someone observes that the color of the water is reflecting the color of the sky, and people's eyes return to the sky, this time noticing subtleties of coloration they hadn't noticed before.

To elicit these observations, the museum guide is using the most common observation strategy: the use of categories to guide the eye. In its broadest form, this strategy works by instructing the eye to look for certain types of things. The museum guide uses the categories of color, shape, and line. In another discipline the categories might be quite different. For example, physicians use categories to help them recognize typical symptoms of illnesses (skin color, breath odor). Archaeologists use categories to help focus their attention on specific sets of features in a landscape that may indicate the presence of buried artifacts (concavities, ridges). Detectives investigating property theft look for specific kinds of clues to help them identity the thief (tool marks, footprints, fibers).

Categories vary widely across contexts, but their basic purpose is the same: they function as a lens to selectively focus the flow of perception on certain features. They operate at a conscious and unconscious level, and it is impossible to imagine human cognition without them. Categories are at work in the expectations, purposes, and assumptions we bring to any experience, allowing us to "see" certain things rather than others. For example, when the museum visitors entered the gallery of nineteenth-century painting they expected to see paintings, which is exactly what they noticed. They probably also noticed the wooden benches in the middle of the gallery since they had to walk around them. But mainly they were focused on the art on the walls. Some visitors may have also noticed the color of the walls (a creamy beige), and perhaps a few of them noticed details like the exit signs and the scuffed wood of the gallery floor. But probably nobody noticed the shape of the light fixtures high on the ceiling, or the motes of dust in the corner, or the even paces of a museum guard as he walked slowly around the perimeter of the gallery.

Lift your eyes from this page for a moment and look at what's in front of you. You might think you can count the number of things you see. But with millions, if not billions, of visual stimuli flooding your eye in any given moment it's impossible for the mind to consciously process all the visual information that comes its way. It is essential to have a filtering mechanism. Otherwise, we couldn't walk across the room without being overwhelmed. But as much as we depend on the mind's workaday unconscious filtering, so too can we consciously overlay it with category strategies to direct the flow of our attention to things we might otherwise overlook. For example, if the museum guide were to ask her visitors to intentionally *try* to notice the color of the walls, or the dress of other visitors in the gallery, or the quality of light, or any number of other things, they could easily do so. But this shift of attentional focus would come at a price: by looking at these things the visitors would probably be paying much less attention to the paintings.

The thing is, we can't be aware of everything we see (although, as I'll discuss in a moment, there can be strategic benefit in trying to do so). Selective attention is a powerful force. We can select what we choose to look at, but doing so necessarily blinds us to other things. One thing that may alter this system is surprise. When something surprising enters our visual field, we often have the sensation of "just seeing it," without having to shift our expectations in order to discern it. For instance, surely our museum visitors would notice if a clown on stilts walked through the gallery, even if they are focused on looking at the paintings. Or would they? It might depend on how intently they are looking for colors, shapes, and lines.

Sometimes our gaze is so fixed on looking for a certain type of thing that we can be astoundingly blind to things outside of our attentional focus. A dramatic example of this comes from the work of cognitive scientist Daniel Simons and his colleague Christopher Chabris. A number of years ago, Simons donned a gorilla suit and the two psychologists conducted an experiment that has become a bit of a sensation. Here's how it goes: subjects are asked to watch a short video of six people wandering around passing basketballs to each other. Three people are wearing black shirts, three are wearing white shirts. The task is to count the number of passes the people in white shirts make. There's a lot of walking and passing going on and it takes some concentration to focus on the white-shirted people (hint: category). Midway through the video, a gorilla walks into the midst of the perambulating people. He pauses to face the camera, thumps his chest, and then strolls off screen. Incredibly, when the experiment was first conducted at Harvard University in 1999—before the video had gone viral—half of the viewers who were focused on the counting task didn't even see the gorilla.[1]

The categories we use to focus our attention profoundly shape what we see. They also shape what we think. Consider the categories that the museum guide chose. Color, shape, and line are certain formal elements of a painting. While the specificity of these categories seems to do a good job of getting visitors to slow down and look carefully, their selectivity also communicates ideas about value and importance. So are these the "right" categories to use when looking at art? It's a good question to ask, even if there isn't a right answer. For example, a formalist art theorist might argue that the museum guide's strategy is inadequate because it fails to guide the eye to other important formal features of the painting, such as scale and proportion or the geometrical organization of the canvas. Another scholar might argue that a strategy for looking closely at art shouldn't begin by emphasizing formal elements at all, but instead should direct people's attention to the story the painting is trying to tell. Yet another scholar might argue that what's important is to look at features in the work that show the cultural influence of the time and social context in which the painting was made.

Debates about which category systems should guide observation don't always get settled easily or at all. But sometimes a set of categories advances the observational practice in a field so rapidly that they quickly become standard practice. Turning to science, a good example comes from the work of Joseph Grinnell, the first director of the Museum of Vertebrate Biology at University of California at Berkeley, and one of the developers of the idea of the "ecological niche". In his early training as an ornithologist in the late 1800s, Grinnell travelled widely to observe birds and other animals in their natural habitats, and he recorded his observations in field notes. Following the note-taking conventions of the time, his notes consisted of lengthy lists that recorded the names of species and number of birds seen, but not much else. Though this was standard practice in the field, Grinnell came to realize that limiting the scope of his field notes to two categories—species and number—discouraged observers from paying close attention to other important features, such as weather and habitat. So Grinnell developed a more rigorous system that required note taking in numerous categories. The system, which he required his assistants to use scrupulously, encouraged the collection of much richer environmental data than had been previously collected, and his method is often credited with fueling the huge growth of environmental field research in the United States in the early twentieth century. More than a century later, the "Grinnellian Method" is still standard practice for many naturalists today.

Open Inventories

Grinnell's field notes have been preserved and made available for study by the Museum of Vertebrate Zoology at the University of California at

Berkeley. Scholar Cathryn Carson has examined them closely and notes an interesting change over time.[2] She observes that when Grinnell first established his method, he followed it fairly rigorously. Over the years, however, his notes became more relaxed to include extensive subjective descriptions and wide-ranging observations. As a mature scientist, Grinnell came to believe that it was impossible to know in advance what would be important to science in the future, and his later notes reflect this. Though he always required his assistants to adhere strictly to the note-taking system he developed, in later years he expanded the system to require extra notebook pages for capturing seemingly unimportant observations. In other words, his technique was this: use a set of categories to look thoroughly for certain kinds of things; then, write down everything else you see, just in case. He had good foresight: today, scientists are examining the notes of Grinnell and his associates for clues about contemporary climate change—something Grinnell could not have anticipated.

Observation strategies are *heuristics*—rules of thumb to be applied when they are useful and set aside when they are not. Like observers of scientific phenomena, connoisseurs of art understand this well. Janos Scholz was a renowned twentieth-century cellist who was almost as famous an art collector as he was a musician. Much of his collection of Italian drawings can now be found at the Morgan Library in New York City, and most of the rest of his vast collection of photographs, prints, and drawings is scattered across well-known museums in the United States. Known for his connoisseur's eye, Scholz wrote about how to observe quality in an artwork. Like our museum guide, Scholz emphasized the use of categories, writing: "Experience will teach the connoisseur to establish a routine for examining various components, like spontaneity of line, imitation of substance, the sensation of visual depth . . . ." But he urges that equally important is "breaking the eye," "[L]ook always at everything, everywhere! This is a cardinal rule, basic and sacred for the connoisseur-curator."[3] Scholz's approach is similar to Grinnell's: use categories to look carefully for certain sorts of features, then go beyond them to notice everything, everywhere.

Of course it is impossible to see "everything, everywhere" in any objective sense. But what the stories of Scholz and Grinnell illustrate is that good observers try to notice as much as they can, in any way they can. Sholz's advice to see "everything, everywhere" captures the spirit of a second broad observation strategy used almost as widely as categories: the making of *open inventories*.

An inventory is an itemized list that aims to record every item of a certain kind or in a certain location. Naturalists take inventories of flora and fauna; businesses take inventories of merchandise. Encyclopedias are

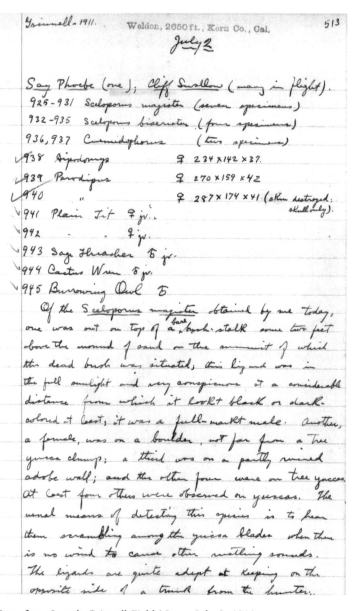

Figure 2.1 Page from Joseph Grinnell Field Notes, July 2, 1911.

With the permission of The Museum of Vertebrate Zoology, University of California, Berkeley.

a kind of inventory, because they aim to comprehensively represent all aspects or instances of a particular kind of thing. Encyclopedic inventories can be narrow in scope, such as a count of owl species in a limited area or an encyclopedia of chess moves. They can also be dazzlingly broad, as in the Encyclopedia of Life, an online initiative with the goal of creating a digital inventory of all the life forms on Earth.[4] Often the entries in an encyclopedia fall easily into a single category (chess openings, life forms). But sometimes they don't, and it is this latter sort of inventory that the term open inventory is meant to capture. Consider the *Encyclopedia Britannica*, which originally aimed to represent the entire range of human knowledge. In the print edition (although not the online version) the entries are arranged alphabetically. This provides an aura of orderliness, but the alphabet is simply a convenient container for wildly heterogeneous content. Open to the "R" pages and you can find entries under Rutabaga, Religion, and Roman road systems.

As an observation strategy, open inventorying eschews categories in favor of taking encyclopedic-like stock of all observable features. Its purpose is to capture the rich, often category-defying jumble of features that make up a whole, and it cultivates a different kind of discriminating perception than the use of categories. Categories help us make perceptual discriminations by directing our attention to certain characteristics of a feature that make it part of a set—the way a circle is part of the set of shapes in a painting, for example. Compiling an open inventory of features draws our attention to the particularity of each individual feature itself, and ultimately to the complex coalescence of disparate features into a larger whole.

What does open inventorying look like in practice? Let's return to our museum tour. After visitors have spent quite a long time with the seascape, the museum guide brings them to another painting in the gallery. The painting shows a pastoral scene of farmland and rolling hills dotted with a few farms. "This time we're going to do something different," she says. "Take a look at this painting. Let's make a list of every single thing we see." The visitors dive right in.

"I see a house," one visitor begins.
"I see people working in the fields."
"I see a farm."
"I see puffy clouds."
"I see a warm day; people don't have coats on and it looks like they're hot."
"I see a lot of white everywhere."
"I see someone—a farmer?—who looks sad."

"I see a picture frame."
"I see a very ornate picture frame; it's gold, with lots of fancy carving."
"I see the artist's signature at the bottom."

The list continues to grow as the visitors discern more and more features of the work. Their observations vary widely in type. Some are about the formal features of the painting (the whiteness of the clouds, the patchwork pattern of the farmland). Some are about the feel of the painting (the warmth of the sun, the sadness of a face). Some are about the story the painting seems to be telling. Some are even about the painting's frame and the artist's signature. While visitors' observations don't parse neatly into categories, the overall inventory they collectively create captures something of the complexity of the painting—the multiple, interacting ways in which the work makes itself vivid and meaningful.

Try This

Looking 10 × 2

1. Look at an image or object slowly for at least 30 seconds. Let your eyes wander.
2. List 10 words or phrases about anything you notice.
3. Repeat steps 1 and 2: look again, and add 10 more words or phrases to your list.

Very important to the process of inventorying is the fact that the visitors are *describing* what they see. Description is an ongoing act of observation, not just a tidy report of a prior internal mental state. When the visitors put their observation into words, it literally helps them see the painting, because the words available to us to describe what we see give form to our perceptions. Actually, to be precise, it's not just words that shape what we see, but any form of symbolic representation. The visitors could be sketching their observations, or expressing them through gestures, or even sounds. No matter what the medium, the form in which they communicate their observations is part of the act of seeing.

This topic—the question of how our modes of communication influence what we see—is the proverbial elephant in the room for a book on slow looking. It can't be escaped: every human description is subjective, so long as it is a subject—a person—doing the describing. There are all kinds of interesting puzzles concerning the relationship between subjectivity and slow look-ing. Later on, in Chapters 7 and 8, we'll take a look at some of these puzzles. For now, I simply want to point to the fact that describing their observations to one another is an important part of the museum visitors' experience.

Another important feature of the visitors' experience is that their many diverse observations coalesce into a whole that is greater than the sum of its parts. The overall inventory the visitors create is *evocative* for them: it evokes a sense of the painting's richness and complexity in a way that any single obser-vation can't, and its totality communicates a sense of immediacy and scope.

Evocativeness is the *modus operandi* of poetry, and poets frequently use inventorying as a powerful descriptive technique. Few poets love a good list as much as Walt Whitman. Here are some lines from stanza 8 of his famous poem, *Song of Myself:*

> The blab of the pave, tires of carts, sluff of boot-soles, talk of the promenaders,
> The heavy omnibus, the driver with his interrogating thumb, the clank of the shod horses on the granite floor,
> The snow-sleighs, clinking, shouted jokes, pelts of snow-balls,
> The hurrahs for popular favorites, the fury of rous'd mobs . . .[5]

Whitman's inventory of a winter scene skates across categories. The incongruent juxtaposition of the "blab of the pave" and "the rumble of the crowd" and the driver's "interrogating thumb" asserts the particularity of each feature, while the profusion of perceptions as a whole conveys the complexity of a world that is jumbled but not random.

In the arts, a sense of jumbled connectedness is the yield of a good open inventory, precisely because it is so evocative and category-hopping. We can see it in the museum visitors' wide-ranging observations as well as in Whitman's lines. Articulating this sensibility in his poem *Windsor-Forest*, Alexander Pope describes the jumble of wild elements in a forest scene, and notes how they hang together,

> Not Chaos like together crush'd and bruis'd,
> But as the world, harmoniously confus'd.

Categories like order. Inventories can be beautifully, harmoniously con-fused. Like poets, many visual artists like harmonious jumbles, too. To choose a familiar example, the so-called "peasant scene" paintings of sixteenth-century Dutch artist Pieter Bruegel offer exuberant visual inventories of a wide sweep of activities at a single moment in village life.

Open inventories often have a collage-like quality, and artists who favor this strategy sometimes use collage as a medium. Works like *The Dove* by Romare Bearden use collage to depict a profusion of images and activities that capture the immediacy of an urban street scene. (A full-color version of this work can easily be found online. I encourage you to take a look. We will come back to this work again in Chapter 8 and spend more time with it.)

Robert Rauschenberg's series of found-object *Combines* take collage into three dimensions and feel inventory-like in the way they bring together a host of distinct elements to create a sense of immediacy. With a double use of the strategy, they communicate a sense of jumbled connectedness, and are themselves a physical instance of open inventory, comprised as they are of wildly disparate objects—a stuffed Angora goat, a tire, printed images, paint splotches, battered strips of wood.

Most of the examples in this chapter focus on visual perception, since it is the mode of observation I'm most familiar with. But the broad principles and techniques discussed here apply to other senses as well—touch, sound, smell, and even taste. This is nowhere more important than

Figure 2.2 Romare Bearden. *The Dove*. 1964.

Art © Romare Bearden Foundation, Inc./Licensed by VAGA, New York, NY.

Digital Image © The Museum of Modern Art/Licensed by SCALA/Art Resource, NY.

for the strategy of open inventory, an observation strategy that emphasizes gathering perceptions from "everything, everywhere." For example, a park ranger I know takes groups of schoolchildren into a swamp in the Everglades National Park in Florida and has them use an auditory version of the Looking 10 × 2 strategy described on the previous page. First they close their eyes and listen for ten different sounds; then they share what they hear with one another, pausing to listen for the various hums, whines, whistles, clickety-thumps, splashes, and buzzings that each of them mentions. Then they repeat the cycle, always amazed to discover how much more there is to hear the second time around.

With regard to the senses, open inventory isn't necessarily just a matter of capturing all the impressions your senses convey; it can also include techniques for enhancing your physical awareness. One repository of wisdom for multi-sensory observation is in the techniques people use to track animals—a human endeavor that greatly depends on slow looking for its success. Suppose you're a wildlife photographer, moving carefully and silently through the forest, trying to detect signs of wildlife. Here's a tip from Princeton University's Outdoor Action Guide to Nature Observation & Stalking: "Intentionally vary your sensory awareness. Vary your vision. Pay intermittent attention to your environment. Shift your focus. Flash back and forth through your various senses, vision, hearing, smell, touch, and taste."[6]

Returning to the visual, another open inventory technique drawn from animal tracking, splatter vision, is considered by nature guides to be the best way to detect subtle movement in the natural environment. Also used by police to scan the movement of crowds, splatter vision involves letting your vision "spread out" in soft focus over a wide range, without focusing on anything in particular. Although things will look fuzzy, the eye is surprisingly sensitive to movement in this mode; once you detect some movement, such as the shiver of a leaf as a bird takes flight, or the downward tug of a blade of grass as a small animal passes underneath, you can quickly focus in on it.[7]

The two broad strategies we have been exploring so far—categorizing, and the making of open inventories—are by far the most widely used strategies for slow looking. Practices that involve focusing the eye on certain types of things (categories), and practices that involve casting a wide net to capture a range of observations (open inventory), can be found at work in any field of study or human endeavor that involves empirical observation. Moreover, they are complementary: each strategy's strength serves as a kind of corrective to the other's weakness. What makes them strategies for slow looking is that they provide a structure for going beyond a quick glance in order to prolong and deepen observation.

Try This

Splatter Vision

Try this outdoors in a natural environment: a woodland, a park, maybe your own backyard.

- Look at the horizon and soften your gaze. Hold your arms straight out to both sides of you and start wiggling your fingers. Gradually bring your arms forward until you can first detect movement. This is your lateral field of vision.
- Now put one arm straight up and one straight down. Do the same from top to bottom; this is your vertical field of vision.
- Now rest your arms by your side, keep your eyes soft, and stand still. See what out-of-the-ordinary movements in the environment you notice.

Two additional and widely used observation strategies also deserve mention. In fact they are so well known to most of us that they scarcely seem like strategies at all. But labeling them as such helps disembed them from the flow of cognition and makes them more available for study and purposeful use. The first is *scale and scope*.

Scale and Scope

This strategy, which has to do with adjusting physical perspective, tends to work alongside the strategies of categorization and open inventorying, rather than in contrast with them. Making adjustments of scale and scope is such common practice that we hardly think of it as strategic. But it functions as a strategy for slow looking by providing techniques to focus the eye and prolong observation.

Techniques of scale and scope involve altering our distance from things, or adjusting our breadth of view, in order to bring certain features into relief. Instruments such as cameras, microscopes, and telescopes can play a role, although our bodies alone often suffice—for instance, when we simply move in close to something, or stand far back, in order to gain a new physical perspective.

The advent of the microscope, and later microphotography, provided powerful tools for close-up viewing—a classic scale-and-scope strategy. In a lovely combination of prolonged observation, evanescence, and ingenuity, a man named Wilson Bentley made a life's work of this. Known as "the snowflake man," he was born in 1865 in the small town of Jericho, Vermont, where he lived and worked his entire life as a farmer and scientist. At a young age he became fascinated with the crystal structure of snowflakes, and eventually he devised a sophisticated method for studying them that combined a microscope with a camera. His technique

Figure 2.3 Wilson Bentley. Plate XIX of *Studies Among the Snow Crystals*. From *Annual Summary of the Monthly Weather Review*. 1902.

Credit: National Oceanic & Atmospheric Administration (NOAA).

was to capture a snowflake on a chilled velvet surface, carefully photograph it in a cold backyard shed using equipment he had specially designed to be used with warmly mittened hands, and then process the photograph in such a way as to bring out the white snowflake against a dark background. Over the course of his life he produced over five thousand images of snowflakes and made many original discoveries about their crystalline structure.

Bentley was also interested in the beauty of snowflakes, which he frequently stressed in public lectures about his work, and he viewed his photographs as artistic as well as scientific. Artists, too, use strategies of scale and scope to look slowly and carefully at the world, and through their works encourage us to do the same. For example, contemporary artist Vija Celmins uses close-up scale along with narrow scope in her stunningly detailed images of the surface of waves, drawing attention to the fluid geometry of moving water.

In his well-known work, *The Earth from Above*, photographer Yves Arthus-Bertrand takes wide-scope pictures from above the earth that draw attention to painterly patterns of topography indiscernible at ground level.

Figure 2.4 Vija Celmins. *Untitled (Ocean)*. 1970. Graphite on acrylic ground on paper, 14¼ × 18⅞ inches.

Collection of The Museum of Modern Art, New York.

One of my favorite examples comes from the work of artist Chuck Close. He paints oversized, seemingly pixelated portraits made up of shapes within shapes that cleverly require viewers to make their own physical adjustments of scale: one must stand at a distance from the painting in order to bring the overall subject into focus, and stand close to it to see how the individual shapes form a grid. (A full-color version of this work can easily be found online. I encourage you to take a look.)

How might our museum guide use strategies of scale and scope with the visitors? The most straightforward thing she can do is to have them change their physical perspective. For example, she could ask them to sit or lie on the floor and look up at a sculpture. Or she could ask them to stand close to a painting and describe how it looks when their eyes are 6 inches away (a surprisingly revealing activity). A common strategy of

Figure 2.5 Chuck Close. *Self-Portrait*, 1997. Oil on canvas, 102 × 84 inches (259.1 × 213.4 cm).

Photograph by Ellen Page Wilson, courtesy Pace Gallery.

scope involves using a frame. It can be the frame of a camera lens, the frame around a painting, or the frame you peer through by creating a circle with your hands. Accordingly, the guide might provide visitors with a cardboard viewfinder, or ask them to make a scope with their thumb and forefinger and isolate a section of a painting to describe in detail. Any of these strategies will encourage slow looking by providing a structure for visitors to go beyond a first glance.

Juxtaposition

The final observation strategy I'll mention is *juxtaposition*, which consists simply of placing objects next to each other with the purpose of bringing forward certain features through comparison. Like the strategy of scale and scope, it is so common that it almost defies being called a strategy. But it functions strategically when we purposefully juxtapose objects in order to more clearly see the specific features of each one. Whenever you arrange objects on a shelf with an eye toward how they complement one another, you're using the strategy of juxtaposition.

A straightforward example of this strategy at work in science occurs in the fields of zoology and botany. In their research collections, scientists juxtapose specimens of fauna or flora in order to discern differences and similarities between species. Museums, of course, are repositories of collections, and the strategic juxtaposition of objects is a linchpin of museum display. Whether it is a collection of plant specimens or paintings or potsherds, the adjacencies of objects are usually designed by curators to draw visitors' attention to particular features. Often the difference between juxtaposed objects is easily discernible, such as in an exhibition of different paintings by the same artist, or by different artists in the same region or era. But juxtaposition can be strategically used to draw attention to subtle differences as well.

A clever display in the Art of the Americas wing of the Museum of Fine Arts in Boston shows a row of eighteenth-century chairs. The chairs are all made in the exact same style, and at first glance they look almost identical. But upon close inspection, and with some gentle encouragement from a wall placard, one begins to notice subtle ways in which different cabinetmakers interpreted the features of a standard design. For example, all the chairs have ball and claw feet—a common design of the time in which the foot of the chair leg consists of a carved bird claw clasping a wooden ball in its talons. One cabinetmaker favors a tightly gripped claw that seems to cause the ball to bulge between the talons. Another shows the claw resting lightly on the ball, as if the bird had just alighted there.

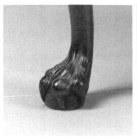

Figure 2.6 1. Chair [detail]; English, about 1750–60. Mahogany, beech. Overall: 94.6 × 59.1 × 48.9 cm (37¼ × 23¼ × 19¼ inches). Museum of Fine Arts, Boston. Gift of Mrs. Joshua Crane Sr. in memory of her husband, 30.726.

2. Side chair [detail]; about 1765–85. Object Place: Boston, Massachusetts. Mahogany, soft maple, red oak. Overall: 97.2 × 62.5 × 47.9 cm (38¼ × 24⅝ × 18⅞ inches). Museum of Fine Arts, Boston. Gift of Priscilla Quincy Weld in memory of her mother and grandmother, Ruth Draper Peters and Alice Ames Draper, and Elizabeth Marie Paramino Fund in memory of John F. Paramino, Boston Sculptor, Arthur Tracy Cabot Fund, Ernest Kahn Fund, John Wheelock Elliott and John Morse Elliott Fund, Alice M. Bartlett Fund, and Edwin E. Jack Fund, 1996.52.

3. Side chair [detail]; about 1770. Object Place: Salem, Massachusetts. Attributed to: Nathaniel Gould, American, 1734–81. Mahogany, maple, pine. 93.3 × 56.5 × 45.7 cm (36¾ × 22¼ × 18 inches). Museum of Fine Arts, Boston. Museum purchase with funds by exchange from Gift of Mary W. Bartol, John W. Bartol, and Abigail W. Clark, Gift of Dr. and Mrs. Thomas H. Weller, Bequest of Mrs. Stephen S. FitzGerald, Bequest of Dr. Samuel A. Green, Gift of Gilbert L. Steward, Jr., Gift of Mrs. Daniel Risdon, Gift of Miss Elizabeth Clark in memory of Mary R. Crowninshield, Gift of Mrs. Clark McIlwaine, Gift of Mr. and Mrs. Russell W. Knight-Collection of Ralph E. and Myra T. Tibbetts, Gift of Elizabeth Shapleigh, Gift of Miss Harriet A. Robeson, Gift of the John Gardner Greene Estate, Bequest of Barbara Boylston Bean, Gift of Miss Catherine W. Faucon, Gift of Jerrold H. Barnett and Joni Evans Barnett, and Gift of Dr. Martha M. Eliot, 2004.2062.

Photographs © 2017 Museum of Fine Arts, Boston.

Discerning this distinction leads to more discoveries, and soon, through juxtaposition, what initially looked like a bland grouping of chairs becomes quite intriguing.

The group of visitors that our museum guide is shepherding probably has museum fatigue by now. But supposing they are refreshed after a quick snack in the museum cafeteria, how might the museum guide use juxtaposition as a strategy to help them look at a few more paintings? The possibilities are numerous and known to any educator who instructs through the use of comparisons. For instance, the visitors could identify two paintings that seem alike, then describe how their features are similar and different. They could look at a particular gallery as a whole and look for similar and different features across all the works. They could propose their own juxtapositions by identifying two or three paintings they'd like to place next to one another, and explain why. Each of these strategies would work. But the museum closes at 5:00 PM. It's time for the tour to end.

Strategy Anatomy

The observation strategies I've discussed in this chapter—*categories, open inventory, scale and scope,* and *juxtaposition*—are broadly applicable to all kinds of contexts. They are used by experts in advanced fields of study to make sophisticated observations, and they are used by all of us, young and old, in many settings in everyday life. For all their breadth, the strategies offer concrete, actionable guidelines. The use of categories tells the eye where to look. Making an open inventory provides a structure for capturing a jumble of perceptions. Altering the scale and scope of perception helps the eye see things from fresh perspectives. Juxtaposing objects makes subtle features discernible by bringing forward similarities and differences.

While each strategy has its own flavor, they all share two important features. The first is that they encourage people to go beyond first glance and to look at one thing closely, whether it is a painting, a patch of the natural world, a historical artifact, or an object from everyday life. Time is a precious human resource, and we should be prepared to spend it lavishly if we want to cultivate people's capacity for slow looking. Consider the museum guide's choice: instead of giving visitors a tour of the entire museum, making sure to point out its many highlights, as perhaps they expected, she resisted expectations and gave them ample—really ample—time to look.

A second, more technical feature of the strategies discussed in this chapter is that they provide what educators sometimes call "scaffolding", rather than stepwise instructions. Instructions tell you what to do; scaffolds support you so you can do something on your own. The strategies discussed here encourage people to make their own discerning perceptions rather than to corroborate what experts tell them they should see. This is more than a motivational nicety: when people look slowly at things for themselves, they tend to grasp complexities and make connections in a way that no amount of expert information can convey. This is one of the reasons that slow looking is a unique mode of learning. This theme—the connection between slow looking and an appreciation of complexity—is explored in depth in Chapter 8. To begin to set the stage, the next chapter offers some real-life stories about the practice of slow looking in four quite different educational settings.

Notes

1 You can find the video on YouTube, but reading about it here will have spoiled it for you; you'll almost certainly see the gorilla: https://www.youtube.com/watch?v=vJG698U2Mvo.
2 Carson, C. (2007, Feb.). Writing, writing, writing: The natural history field journal as a literary text. The Doreen B. Townsend Center for the Humanities. Retrieved from http://townsendcenter.berkeley.edu/article11.shtml.
3 Scholz, J. (1960). Connoisseurship and the training of the eye. *College Art Journal* 19(3), 226–230.
4 See http://eol.org/.
5 Whitman, W. (1892). Song of Myself. Retrieved from https://www.poetry foundation.org/poems-and-poets/poems/detail/45477.
6 Curtis, R. (1999). Outdoor action guide to nature observation & stalking. Outdoor Action Program, Princeton University. Retrieved from http://www.princeton.edu/~oa/nature/naturobs.shtml.
7 Ibid.

CHAPTER 3

Slow in Practice

On January 10, 2013, journalist and National Geographic Fellow Paul Salopek set out on a slow and very long walk. His path began in Herto Bouri, Ethiopia, a site where some of the world's oldest human fossils have been found, and it follows the ancient pathways of human migration—the walkways our ancestors traveled as they dispersed from Africa and spread out across the world. At this writing, Paul is in his fifth year of walking. His project, called *Out of Eden Walk*, is a storytelling project.[1] Over the course of a decade he will walk more than 21,000 miles—out of Africa, through the Middle East and into the Caucasus, along the silk road through Asia, up into Russia and the Arctic, and then down the entire coast of the Americas—until the journey's end in Tierra del Fuego, the last corner of the continental world to be settled by humans approximately 12,000 years ago.

Paul walks with local walking partners; he doesn't hurry. He writes and posts regular dispatches on the project's website. His reporting tells today's stories through the prisms of both the deep past and hidden-in-plain-view present. This chapter draws on Paul's walk to explore two practices related to slow looking. The first is a practice called slow journalism—a radical alternative to the fast-paced, daily cycle of ever-breaking news. The second is an educational program related to Paul's walk in which young people around the globe practice slow looking in their local neighborhoods and online with each other.

Paul devised *Out of Eden Walk* as an experiment in slow journalism, but he is no stranger to the fast-paced news cycle. A foreign correspondent and two-time Pulitzer Prize winner, he spent a couple of decades covering world news hotspots. Yet he says "slow" is in his bones, and he has always been drawn to it. "I took a profession that values speed over almost anything else—accuracy too, but also speed—and somehow bent it to the pace of my own life."[2]

Paul's foot level speed these days is approximately three miles per hour. It suits him. As he explains in one of his *Out of Eden Walk* dispatches:

> Walking across the Earth, I have relearned the old ceremony of departures and arrivals. (Making and striking campsites, packing and unpacking rucksacks, an antique and comforting ritual.) I have absorbed landscapes through my taste buds, by gleaning farmers' harvests. And I have reconnected with fellow human beings in ways I could never conceive as a reporter crisscrossing maps by jet and car. Out walking, I constantly meet people. I cannot ignore them or drive by them. I greet them. I chat with strangers five, ten, twenty times a day. I am engaged in a meandering, three-mile-an-hour conversation that spans two hemispheres. In this way walking builds a home everywhere.[3]

Paul's version of slow journalism is extreme. But among journalists he isn't alone: the small but growing slow journalism movement is based on the simple premise that thoughtful, accurate, compelling journalistic storytelling takes time. Paul's version is ambulatory. Other journalists immerse themselves in a location for weeks, months, even years at a time. Still others stay home, turning a slow lens on local people and places. For example, a lovely instance of local slow journalism is *One in 8 Million*, a 54-story series published in the *New York Times* over the course of a year.[4] Each story consists of a 3-minute miniature portrait of an everyday New Yorker. The stories are told through a slow sequence of black and white photographs by photographer Todd Heisler, accompanied by excerpts of an interview with the person. We hear the voices of a jury clerk, an animal rescuer, a bar fighter, a wedding wardrober, a mayoral maid, an accountant, an only child, a sports fan. The stories are brief, but unhurried. Photographs and voice come together to create the feeling that one has truly lingered for a time with each individual.

Slow journalism can take many forms: it can be text-based articles, or multimedia essays; it can include photography, video, and audio. It can be long-form journalism that draws readers deeply and expansively into the complexities of a topic; it can be short- or medium-form reporting that immerses audiences in small moments and experiences. But regardless of the form it takes, it has a distinctive flavor. Several years ago when the term "slow journalism" was just coming into use, journalist Mark Berkey-Gerard took stock of the various ways it was described in print and offered a provisional definition that still resonates today. He writes:

Slow journalism:
- Gives up the fetish of beating the competition.
- Values accuracy, quality, and context, not just being fast and first.
- Avoids celebrity, sensation, and events covered by a herd of reporters.
- Takes time to find things out.
- Seeks out untold stories.
- Relies on the power of narrative.
- Sees the audience as collaborators.[5]

As Berkey-Gerard's definition suggests, slow journalism is not scoop-driven. Nor does it have the rapid-fire, pseudo-objective tone of what's typically called hard news. It is based on the belief that most stories neither begin nor end with a headline: they permeate the real lives of people and communities, and they take time to uncover. Rob Orchard, a popular spokesperson for slow journalism and editor of *Delayed Gratification*, a magazine wholly devoted to its practice, explains in a TedX talk that slow journalism is "about being right, not being first," and that ultimately "it's about taking your time to do something of quality."[6]

Like slow looking, slow journalism is about uncovering more than first meets the eye. Slowness, in this sense, isn't about maintaining a prescribed pace, it is about taking what the scholar and multimedia journalist Benjamin Ball calls "proper time":

> Slow journalism is not about reaching a particular word-count, duration, or production time, but about reaching an audience, and not only reaching an audience *technically*, but also, and more importantly, engaging the audience intellectually and emotionally. "Slow" describes the extent and moral tenor of the communicative process, rather than its duration or tempo.[7]

Ball's remark points out that "slow" works in two ways. As a journalistic practice it is the careful looking and listening slow journalists do in order to produce a nuanced story. But slow is also practiced by audiences, because slow journalism invites audiences to linger in a story or a scene and inhabit it for a bit—such as, photo essays in *One in 8 Million* allow us to dwell momentarily but unhurriedly inside the lives of everyday New Yorkers.

For Paul Salopek, the "proper time" of his slow journalism varies in both length and form. His written dispatches for *Out of Eden Walk*—posted roughly every 2 weeks—are typically between 600–1,000 words.

In "The Things They Leave Behind," he of tells the story of migrant workers walking by night through the Afar desert toward the Red Sea, with the hope of gaining work in the Middle East. In "Electronic Oasis," he brings us inside the world of a young Ethiopian technician and his makeshift desert charging station, where nomads can come with their camels and cargo to recharge their cell phones for a few cents. In "It's Always 1989 in a Forgotten Caucasus Village," he pauses in a once-bustling town that is now scattered with empty farmhouses to take tea with an administrator at the last Soviet-style farm in Azerbaijan.

In addition to producing regular dispatches, Paul also experiments in slow journalism through very short form media, contradictory though this may sound. Every 100 miles along the walk, Paul pauses to create what he calls a "milestone"—a record of the landscape and a person he meets nearby. A milestone consists of several elements, each of which is quite short but that together draw a reader into a slow, immersive experience of time and place. First there is simply a photo of the place, along with a two- or three-sentence introduction, and the geographic coordinates. Then there is a 360-degree scrollable photographic panorama Paul takes while turning slowly in one spot, along with a photograph of the sky above his head and the earth below. There is a one minute video "glance" that captures whatever is in the immediate visual and aural environment—wind in the desert, rain on asphalt, footsteps in dry grass, the growl of a farm tractor. Finally, there is a picture of the first person Paul encounters within six miles of the spot, along with a brief interview. He always asks the same three questions: Who are you? Where do you come from? Where are you going? Here is his encounter with a 22-year-old migrant farm worker at milestone twenty-one of the walk, near Pyla, Cyprus.[8]

Who are you?
I am named Jaskarah.

Where do you come from?
Nawanshahr. It is in the Punjab, India. Cyprus is a very nice country. I have two or three friends here who work on the farm. I come to work. Money.

Where are you going?
After one more year, I go home. I want to open my own shop. A clothing shop. This is my dream.

These milestones create a collage of very short moments, drawing readers into a slow experience of time and place that is deeply local. But they are also global in several ways: each is part of a worldwide string of milestones that Paul is creating as he walks across the globe; each milestone has a global audience, and most, in some way, resonate with people across geographical and cultural boundaries. This theme, of connecting people globally by slowly exploring the local, is a through line of Paul's journalistic work. It is also a theme that links his *Out of Eden Walk* project to an online global educational program for young people.

Paul and Project Zero

In the fall of 2012, during the final months of preparation for his walk, Paul wondered if there might be an educational component connected to his project. Although he insists he is not an educator himself, he knew the walk would be a learning journey for him, and he wondered whether it might serve a similar purpose for young people. He didn't have a specific idea in mind, but he knew what he *didn't* want: a didactic program that delivered geography or world history lessons using his dispatches as required texts. Instead, he wanted something that shared the spirit of the walk's philosophy. He asked around about possible partners, and by happy coincidence his trail took him to Project Zero, a research organization at Harvard Graduate School of Education with a long history of innovative educational projects. It also happens to be where I work.

I remember the first time my colleagues and I met Paul. He had sent us an intriguing note about the project he was preparing to undertake, and we invited him to our offices to tell us a bit more about it. When he arrived, we gathered in a small office around a slim, serious man, slightly hunched over a laptop, with a spellbinding story to tell. After a few conversations, it became clear that there was a strong resonance between Paul's vision for *Out of Eden Walk*, and Project Zero's ideas about learning. Specifically, we shared a deep belief in the value of slow looking and attentive listening, a commitment to the importance of learning through stories, and a passionate interest in encouraging meaningful dialogue across geography and culture.

In another fortunate occurrence, a small and forward-thinking philanthropic organization called The Abundance Foundation got wind of our meeting of minds, and joined the conversation. Directed by Stephen Kahn, The Abundance Foundation supports educational work in the areas of health, intercultural exchange, and the arts. Kahn, an emergency medicine physician with a strong interest in global youth empowerment, saw potential in a collaboration between *Out of Eden Walk* and Project Zero, and agreed to support the development of an educational initiative. Thus, the seed for what would eventually become the Out of Eden Learn program was sown. Three researchers at Project Zero came together to conceptualize and build the program, and each brought with them a particular focus. Liz Dawes Duraisingh came to the project with a background in history teaching and a special interest in how to help young people connect their own life stories to larger human stories. Carrie James, a sociologist by training, brought a strong background in investigating the civic and moral dimensions of young people's online interactions. I came to the project with a background in developing programs to teach thinking and—no surprise—with an interest in slow looking.

Now in its fifth year, Out of Eden Learn is an online cultural exchange program that connects students around the world. It uses the leitmotif of Paul's walk, but it isn't itself a journalism program. Instead, it's inspired by the themes that intersect slow journalism with Project Zero ideas about learning. Its three primary goals are to encourage students to: 1) slow down to observe the world carefully and to listen attentively to others; 2) exchange stories and observations about people, place, and identity; and 3) reflect on how their own lives connect to bigger human stories.

Like Paul's walk, Out of Eden Learn has struck a chord with its audience. At this writing, over twenty thousand students in over one thousand classrooms across fifty-seven countries have participated in the program. The program works like this: classrooms from around the world are clustered into small, diverse learning groups—we call them "walking parties"—that undertake a 12-week curriculum together. Students in preschool through high school participate in the program, and each walking party is made up of about eight similarly-aged classrooms, which are intentionally chosen for their geographic, cultural, and socioeconomic diversity. The curriculum consists of weekly activities connected to the aforementioned themes. Students take slow walks through their neighborhoods and document things they'd like to share with other students. They conduct interviews, listen to neighbors' stories, explore connections between their own communities and the wider world, and investigate contemporary global issues. They post about their work on the Out of Eden Learn online platform, where they share perspectives and ideas with other students in their walking party. The program is free of charge, and teachers are creative in how they adapt it to their classrooms, using it in a wide variety of teaching contexts, including preschool and elementary school classrooms, English language and literature courses, weekly technology classes, lunchtime or after school enrichment clubs, and regular history and social studies lessons.

From the standpoint of slow looking, the Out of Eden Learn program is distinctive in that it invites students to explore human culture, first by looking slowly and closely at their own surroundings—their neighborhoods, the everyday objects and people around them—and then by bringing that quality of slow to their online interactions with other youth in their walking parties. Importantly, Out of Eden Learn doesn't ask youth to forsake their cellphones and computers in favor of slowing down. (Just as Paul Salopek does not forsake electronics, nor do most slow journalists.) Instead, it invites them to do what slow journalists do: use whatever media suits their purpose—from pictures and video to pencil and paper—to observe and describe what they see.

When my colleagues and I developed Out of Eden Learn, we recognized that the emphasis on slow was at odds with what students typically experience in school, but we hoped that students would find the slow-centered activities engaging. We didn't anticipate how eagerly they would take to them. It turns out that young people across the globe seem to be quite hungry for slow. In words that could have come from any number of students, a 12-year-old says: "When you slow down and pay more attention there is a whole new world around you." A 14-year-old reports: "It's really amazing what things can look like when you just take the time to look for them." Yet another student observes:

> People in this modern age rarely ever just slow down and look around them. Obviously, you shouldn't do that in the middle of the road, but in other places you can, like the park! Unfortunately, the world is always rushing and moving, never slowing down just to see the wonderful world they're in.[9]
>
> (Age 10, Accra, Ghana)

These sentiments stand in stark contrast to a common narrative about the accelerated pace of contemporary life and young people's woefully short attention spans. People often complain that students' lives are so glutted and fueled by fast-paced media—particularly social media—that they have no interest in slowing down. Except that in the Out of Eden Learn program, apparently they do. Which raises the question: what's going on?

One can speculate about the answer to this question—and my colleagues and I certainly have—but at Project Zero we are educational researchers by trade, so it was natural for us to seek a research-based answer as well. We realized that we had two relevant data sources that could help. The first was the results of an online survey that all students take once they have completed the Out of Eden Learn program. The survey asks a series of general questions about students' impressions of the program, and students often mention slow looking in their answers. (The quotes in the previous paragraph, for example, came from the student surveys.) The second source was the actual work students posted on the Out of Eden Learn platform when they were engaged in the project's slow-focused activities, such as the pictures and accompanying comments they posted about taking neighborhood walks and documenting the everyday. We decided to look closely at both these data sources. The student surveys could tell us what students *say* about slow; the analysis of student work could tell us what students actually *do* when they practice slow looking.

It turns out that there's quite a good match between what students say and what they do. In both strands of research—the student self-report surveys, and the analysis of student work—the data cluster into the same four broad themes. Taken together, these four themes offer a textured picture of what students say they like about slow, and how they are actually experiencing it. The remainder of this chapter offers a glimpse of these research findings.

Slow Four Ways

The four themes are: *seeing with fresh eyes*; *exploring perspective*; *noticing detail*; and *philosophical well-being*. Each theme has a distinctive quality that is conceptually separate from the others and which students themselves recognize as unique. But the themes do overlap. For example, one student slows down to carefully observe her neighborhood and draw an overhead view of it. Her drawing shows that she is noticing subtle details, such as the glow of porch lights at dusk and the moths hovering nearby. Accordingly, her map falls into the noticing detail category. In addition, the student's map shows that she is exploring a unique perspective by taking what she calls a moth's eye view. So the map also falls into the exploring perspective category. But despite the fact that students' responses occasionally fall into more than one category, each theme is conceptually distinct. The following sections explore each theme in turn.

Seeing with Fresh Eyes

> I learned that there are so many different and amazing things around the world and that if we just stop to look around us and take notice we will see all the amazing things just outside of our houses.
>
> (Age 12, Accra, Ghana)

When young people begin to practice slow looking, they commonly experience a sense of suddenly seeing their familiar world with fresh eyes, as if the world around them was being newly unveiled. A high school student in Mumbai walks home from school and notices the details of street scenes he has walked by hundreds of times before—a barber cutting someone's hair, a group of boys playing stickball. A fifth grader in the United States takes a car ride with his father and is startled to notice how many parking lots there are, right there in his neighborhood. A kindergarten student in Piraeus, Greece, bends down with delighted surprise to examine tiny plants sprouting from the cracks in her school playground—a playground she has run and skipped and jumped on every day without noticing before.

Students have no trouble finding words to express this experience. One student puts it like this:

> I have learned to take time to stop whatever I'm doing and look around. I have discovered many things in my neighborhood because of this. I have seen houses I have never seen before and people too. I am usually a very busy person so this helps me discover new things.
>
> (Age 12, Los Angeles, CA, US)

Another student posts a picture online to share with members of his walking party, along with this note:

> This photo really made me think differently about my neighborhood because I never stop and look [and] see what's around me. I also never notice the things that people really don't notice, like rocks.
>
> (Age 10, Chicago, IL, US)

Yet another student writes:

> I used to think that there is usually just one way to look at something. For example, I often go down to the river and look at it. When I looked at it this time I noticed every detail from water spiders to the reflection of trees. . . . There are so many things you can see in one little thing, you just have to look.
>
> (Age 10, West Hartford, CT, US)

As these remarks testify, seeing the world with fresh eyes isn't simply a technical exercise for the students. Instead, they report that they find the experience of walking slowly through their neighborhoods captivating, rewarding, and occasionally even thrilling.

In this they aren't alone. The idea that there is value in seeing the world with fresh eyes is a mainstay of philosophical wisdom and creative practice. Advice abounds about how to do it: make the familiar strange, reframe the everyday, find the hidden in plain view. Such advice has been around for millennia, but humans frequently need to be reminded of it because it addresses a perennial problem of human perception: we need mental concepts and categories in order to make sense of the world, but it is precisely these things that prevent us from seeing the unexpected. As the writer Marcel Proust famously wrote, "The real act of discovery consists not in finding new lands, but in seeing with new eyes."

Exploring Perspective

One way to turn the everyday flow of perception into an act of discovery is to intentionally alter one's angle of view. Students in the Out of Eden Learn program discover this quickly, and it shows up as a major theme in their approach to slow looking. A 10-year-old explains: "When you look at something from a different angle it can be a whole different thing." By way of an example, a 12-year-old reports that "I went across the street and lay on my stomach and took the picture of my house looking up. I was surprised that we had a lot of cool nature and so many leaves!" Another 10-year-old lingers by a fence in her backyard and observes: "If you tilted the camera a certain way it looked like our fence went on forever."

In one of the early activities in the Out of Eden Learn curriculum, students take a slow walk through their neighborhood. Their task is to take photos of things that capture their attention, with an eye toward sharing their photos with their fellow students online. Browsing the students' photographs, it is striking to see the zest with which they explore different physical perspectives. They bend down low to capture swimming koi or the texture of sand. They lean in to focus on the veined lattice-work of a fallen leaf. They climb rooftops to capture an aerial view. They squat down to take a picture of a tiny pebble looming in front of distant hills. They bend over a railing to peer down a stairwell. They snap a shot from the perspective of a bug crawling up a tree. They lie down in the road and look up to capture the geometry of crisscrossing electrical wires overhead. They take close-ups of rocks and bricks, of tree bark and crumpled paper, of the colorful wares of sidewalk vendors. They take distance shots of clouds and prayer flags and traffic jams. They frame the dawn in the rain-slicked surface of an early morning sidewalk.

Figure 3.1
Source: Student, Age 12, Berkeley, California, US.

Often, taking on different physical perspectives leads students to an attitudinal shift in perspective as well. One student climbed to the roof of his school to take a picture, and offered this reflection:

> I took this picture to show how from a different perspective things can look much different. Here I am looking out across my school's campus from a view I have not seen before. From my everyday point of view all I see is the dismal winding road leading towards a busy road, and the graying forest that seems to wrap around the campus. But from up here I can see everything better, I can see farther, I can think of these things from a different mind-set. It makes me kinda think that you need to take account [of] all the different perspectives in life to see how things really are.
>
> (Age 15, Crystal Lake, IL, US)

The student is in a philosophical mood; he seems to be appreciating the "seeing farther" one gets from a shift in mindset. But like many Out of Eden students, he also seems to appreciate that seeing "how things really

Figure 3.2
Source: Student, Age 15, Crystal Lake, Illinois, US.

are" involves not so much seeing the world from one grand perspective but from a kaleidoscope of perspectives. Paul Salopek agrees. As he walks through different countries and terrain, his walk shows us different physical perspectives—most notably a foot-level perspective in a world overrun by motorized transport—and his dispatches invite us to see through the eyes of the people he meets—shopkeepers, artisans, migrant workers, local walking guides, refugees, farmers.

Paul explores perspectives by walking the world, but it can easily happen within a few city blocks. In a lovely blend of walking and looking, the author Alexandra Horowitz takes us on an array of perspective-shifting walks in her book *On Looking*.[10] The book tells the story of eleven different walks she takes, mainly in her native New York City, accompanied by eleven different companions who help her look closely at her surroundings with "expert eyes." In a walk with an urban anthropologist, for example, Horowitz learns to notice the emergent flocking behavior of a group of pedestrians crossing the street at a stoplight (rule: stay with the group, but keep a measured distance from others). In a walk with a geologist, she learns to scrutinize the limestone fronts of office buildings for 300-million-year-old fossilized worm tracks. In a walk around the block with her dog (an expert on being canine), she learns to see the ground-level evidence of recent human and canine activity—the flurry of cigarette butts in front of a commercial building that signal a recent lunch break; the layers of urine splotches at the base of a baluster that reveal traces of other canine commuters. Although Alexandra Horowitz isn't snapping pictures like the students in Out of Eden Learn, she is shifting her angle of view with each new perspective she explores. And through the eyes of each new companion, she discovers another new layer of detail in her city streets.

Noticing Detail

To cap off her experience in the Out of Eden Learn program, a fifth grader in Massachusetts, USA made a short video that consisted of long, lingering shots of several things she had been examining closely—tree bark, stones on a beach, blades of grass, her own image. The student narrated the film herself, and in it she speaks directly to the viewer: "Have you ever looked at something but didn't really see it?" she asks. "We walk by things every day without noticing the details." Echoing the premise of Howoritz's book, this opening remark could have been made by any number of students in Out of Eden Learn. Slow looking is about going beyond a first glance, so it's not surprising that it often involves noticing detail—an experience that students seem to relish. As a 12-year-old from Illinois says, "Every day is an adventure outside because I explore the tiniest things every day." The elaboration of detail can be seductive. In a more extended example, here is a comment made by a 13-year-old to accompany a photograph she shared with other students in her walking party:

> When I stepped out of my house, the first thing that I noticed is various types of colors and patterns on the different gates of the houses. All day our sky is full of birds, as you can see from one of the pictures where the birds came together in one place to make patterns. As you can see all the houses have trees and different type of plants outside their houses. When the sun came out, patterns of different trees form on the roads. When I was about to finish my walk, I was very fascinated by the dainty appearances of fruits stalls and balloons, whose shapes looked similar to fruits too.
>
> (Age 10, Lahore, Pakistan)

The student is describing her photograph, but the description isn't merely after-the-fact reportage; one can sense her noticing more and more detail in the scene even as she describes it. First the patterns in the sky full of birds, then the patterns of tree forms on the road, and then finally, the "dainty appearances of fruits stalls and balloons." This extended description is important, and, as we will see in the next chapter, the act of description is itself a form of slow looking. For students, it is also one of slow looking's most noticeable pleasures. As a 10-year-old student remarks, "You should dig deep down close and notice the tiny little details, because when you do you notice amazing things that if you haven't taken time you wouldn't experience."

It is noteworthy that when students get involved in noticing detail, they often informally use the kind of broad observation strategies discussed in the previous chapter. For example, here is an excerpt from a student who seems to be using an inventorying strategy to observe the details of her smart phone. Listen to how her observations unfold as she compiles her inventory:

> The thing I noticed from this iPhone was that it was rectangular, just the size to fit into a pocket perfectly. It has a circular button in the bottom middle, which is the home button. Its surface is very smooth. At the top middle, there are two circles and, one directly in the middle, a little more above the other and slightly larger. That is the selfie camera. The other circle below is accompanied by rectangle with rounded sides . . .
>
> (Age 13, Singapore, Singapore)

For another example of an observation strategy, here a 10-year-old in Danville, California seems to use the strategy of scale and scope to zoom in and discern new details. She says, "By capturing the bells at a closer angle, it makes me see the details of it, such as the small leafs tinged with pink, and the pearly white color of the bell."

Juxtaposition, yet another strategy discussed in the previous chapter, appears in a Florida student's description of a white orchid she finds in a neighborhood park. She says: "Like a bright star it contrasts with the neutral color of the swamp."

Observations can be made with more than just the eyes, and students often discover details through several of their senses. Here a student uses touch, sound, and sight to poetically capture the multisensory details of taking a swim.

> A soft wind soothes my skin as it passes swiftly through the air. Streets are empty and without any cars. Trees sway as the wind blows into their cramped and compact leaves. The

Figure 3.3
Student, Age 10, Danville, California, US.

ocean is making watery and sizzling sounds as it curls up to my feet. A light breeze brushes against the sand as it cools and settles into the rock solid earth. The water is cold and feels like shards of ice hitting my face. As I get out, the water is chilling and a cold breeze wraps around me as I shiver.

(Age 14, Salem, MA, US)

Is there a typical sequence to slow looking, a natural way in which it tends to unfold? Perhaps. In all the foregoing examples, noticing details seems to flow naturally from seeing things with fresh eyes. Once students' attention is captured, they are easily drawn into a prolonged experience of discernment, noticing small details and differences, identifying features and demarcations, delighting in noticing the astounding specificity of the world around them. This delight in specificity is an adult pleasure as well. Consider the connoisseur's pleasure in making the finest distinctions of the palate or eye; the painter's loving rendering of visual detail; a poet's satisfaction in finding precisely the right word; a journalist's satisfaction in bringing forward the minimal but perfectly evocative details.

The grasses are diverse. Their Kazakh names are *jusan, jabaya, mortik, kuosik, mundalak,* and many others. They are gray-green.

Emerald. Lemon-colored. Chartreuse. Often they are speckled with flowers.

(Paul Salopek, crossing the Kazakh steppe)[11]

I turned a corner on to a broad street shaded from the sun. A generator was sputtering nearby; a siren dopplered across the horizon, the toenails of a small dog being dragged out for his constitutional scraped the concrete, other sounds melted into the air.

(Alexandra Horowitz, walking with a blind woman in New York City)[12]

Philosophical Well-being

The fourth and final theme related to students' experience of slow has a somewhat different quality than the three discussed so far, although its resonances can easily be heard: it is philosophical well-being. Put simply, students report that slowing down reminds them of what's important in life. Frequently they connect slow looking with a feeling of peacefulness. For example, one student from Beaverton, Oregon reflects on her neighborhood walk and says: "Everything is alive and coming together to make the world peaceful and calming, even if it's only for a couple minutes as you walk through it." A student from Baltimore reports: "It was so peaceful to be outside and wandering the neighborhood; it really is nice when you slow down and take a look around you." Relatedly, students often reflect that slow offers an antidote to technology. "Leave your cellphone for some minutes," a student from Sao Paulo, Brazil advises, "it's good to refresh your mind." A Californian observes: "I have learned that maybe when you are sitting in a car on a long road trip, you shouldn't be looking down at your phone, you should be looking out the window."

For many students, slow looking brings about a sense of well-being through an experience of nature. Indeed, it is striking the degree to which nature figures into students' ideas about slow. In every corner of the Out of Eden Learn platform—on five continents, in every grade, in rural and urban settings—students relish taking pictures of the natural world around them. Their comments and photos indicate that they find nature uplifting, thought-provoking, and above all beautiful. In a typical online post, a student from Adelaide, Australia shares a picture of "some wild daisy flowers growing on the street" and talks about being "amazed by their exuberant vitality." She continues: "Although no one looks after them, they bloom their unique beauty so wonderfully." A student from Serpong, Indonesia reflects that "it is very amazing to think of nature's beauty that no human could create."

As these comments suggest, students' sense of philosophical well-being is frequently connected to finding beauty in nature, and the theme of beauty runs through much of what they say. Often students describe this experience as an act discovery: "When I was walking through my neighborhood I noticed all of the beauty . . . that I have never noticed before, and it really amazed me," a fifth grader says. Another student, reflecting on her experience with the curriculum, says simply: "I have learned . . . that I overlook and miss a lot of the beauty in life and that sometimes it's good to slow down and to observe it."

Not surprisingly, this sense of discovery is often linked to the aspects of slow looking discussed earlier. Students discover beauty by seeing their neighborhood with fresh eyes; by noticing the intricate details of something they usually pass by; by taking a photograph of an everyday scene from an unusual perspective. Importantly, students seem to feel that finding and appreciating beauty is good in and of itself. This may seem obvious, but it is striking to consider it against the backdrop of typical educational activities. A great deal of formal education is about doing activities that involve delayed gratification—studying hard to pass the test, memorizing facts in order to get to big ideas, learning rote procedures in order to get to advanced practices. In contrast, through slow looking, students seem to intuitively feel that learning to see beauty in the world is valuable in and of itself; it needs no further justification, nor is it instrumental to a further end.

A final aspect of students' sense of philosophical well-being is implicit in many of students' foregoing comments: slow looking offers them an opportunity to reflect on their own lives. "I pass by this place every day and I had never stop[ped] to see this beautiful landscape," one student muses. "When you are seeing this you feel free and good with yourself. You can think about your problems and try to solve them." Another student takes a walk in a local forest and reflects: "I'm alone, I can think, talk to myself, and all my problems suddenly have a solution." Yet another observes: "I never really noticed this tree . . . but when I took the pictures I think I might have realized that life is not based on electronics."

Taken together, the various themes that contribute to students' sense of philosophical well-being are striking. Students report that slow looking helps them feel peaceful, notice nature, appreciate beauty, and reflect on what's important in life. To a jaded adult ear these insights might sound sentimental, but it would be disrespectful of students' depth of feeling to dismiss them. Slow looking appears to tap into something deep in students

—a familiar yet new discovery about themselves and the world around them.

Their experience wouldn't be surprising to Carl Honoré, a well-known advocate of slow living and the author of a book titled *In Praise of Slowness*.[13] As Honoré argues, "The great benefit of slowing down is reclaiming the time and tranquility to make meaningful connections—with people, with culture, with work, with nature, with our own bodies and minds."[14] Interestingly, Honoré came to this insight through an experience with his own children. Like many of us, he was living a hurried, fast-paced life. One day he found himself in a bookstore contemplating the purchase of a book of one-minute bedtime stories, thinking that it might help save time when reading to his children at night. As he puts it, "Suddenly it hit me: my rushaholism has got so out of hand that I'm even willing to speed up those precious moments with my children at the end of the day. There has to be a better way, I thought, because living in fast forward is not really living at all. That's why I began investigating the possibility of slowing down."[15] Out of Eden Learn students seem to share this point of view. Giving eloquent voice to thoughts Honoré would surely appreciate, a high school student in Switzerland reflects on a slow walk he took with his class:

> We went for a walk as a group, and I found myself quieter than usual, giving my full attention to the elements surrounding me: the clear air that seems to waft toward us straight from the Alps in the far distance, the damp moisture seeping through the ground after rainfall yesterday and this morning, the clouds that hung in a haze, the birds chirping a bit, and crunch of gravel under my feet. Sometimes, this all becomes a muffled backdrop, quickly disappearing from my focus as my attention is fixed on a list of would-be insistencies: deadlines, meetings, schedules. I remember today that attention is a choice. I can choose to be here, noticing these details. I returned to school with a clearer mind.

A Word About Mindfulness

The slow movement is often linked to mindfulness, a mental state in which one is fully and non-judgmentally aware of the present moment. The pursuit of mindfulness is currently quite popular in contemporary culture, and, like Honoré's ideas about slow, mindfulness is viewed as an antidote to the fractured, harried pace of modern life. Often, ideas about mindfulness are mixed together with Zen philosophy, yoga, meditation, and other practices that cultivate stillness, calm, and focus. These ideas are in the cultural air—and sometimes even in the school curriculum[16]—so it isn't surprising that students pick up on them. As a 14-year-old enthusiastically observes, "The birds chirping in the mornings and evenings, the cool breeze, abundant shadow during the day and the fragrance from the flowers offers you the Zen feeling!"

I am all for mindfulness. I'd like more of it in my own life, and I believe the world would be a better place if there were more of it all around. But while a state of mindfulness sometimes accompanies slow looking, it doesn't need to, and it is important not to collapse the two.

Mindfulness is usually talked about as a characterological virtue—and sometimes as an ethical virtue as well: Its characterological virtue has to do with the mental health one achieves by being fully in the present moment and non-judgmentally accepting the self. Its ethical virtue has to do with achieving a state of mind that is most likely to lead to proper insight and right action. Slow looking, as I define it, is an *epistemic* virtue: its value has to do with gaining knowledge. Knowledge can be pursued mindfully or not, and in terms of its epistemic value, it isn't necessarily better if it is. From an educational standpoint this is an important distinction, because although the idea of slow looking is spiritually less ambitious than mindfulness, it is considerably more inclusive. Recall the characteristics of slow looking discussed earlier in this chapter—seeing with fresh eyes, noticing detail, exploring perspective. Occasionally these activities are accompanied by feelings of tranquility and peace, but often not. Sometimes observations tumble forward in a headlong rush; sometimes new perspectives are startling and even disturbing; sometimes restlessness rather than tranquility drives the process of looking. From the standpoint of teaching, this is important because it means that slow looking isn't successful only when students achieve a mindful mental state. It is successful when young people are given the opportunity and tools to look at the world slowly, simply in order to see more of what's around them. The mood and tempo with which they do so is up to them.

Notes

1   Salopek, P. (2013–2017). Out of Eden Walk. *National Geographic*. Retrieved from http://www.nationalgeographic.org/projects/out-of-eden-walk/.
2   Salopek, P. (2016, December 14). Personal interview.
3   Salopek, P. (2015, December 12). Exploring the world on foot. *The New York Times*. Retrieved from https://www.nytimes.com/2015/12/13/opinion/exploring-the-world-on-foot.html.

4   One in 8 million. (2009). *The New York Times*. Retrieved from http://www.nytimes.com/packages/html/nyregion/1-in-8-million/.

5   Berkey-Gerard, M. (2009, July 29). Tracking the 'slow journalism' movement. *Campfire journalism blog*. Retrieved from http://markberkeygerard.com/?s=slow+journalism&submit=Search.

6   Orchard, R. (2014, October 13). The slow journalism revolution. TEDx Madrid. Retrieved from https://www.youtube.com/watch?v=UGtFXtnWME4.

7   Ball, B. (2016). Multimedia, slow journalism as process, and the possibility of proper time. *Digital Journalism 4*(4), 436.

8   Salopek, P. (2014, July 11). Milestone 21: Cyprus. Out of Eden Walk. *National Geographic*. Retrieved from http://www.nationalgeographic.org/projects/out-of-eden-walk/milestones/2014-07-milestone-21-cyprus.

9   All the student quotes and images in this chapter come from data collected on the Out of Eden Learn project. Students' access to the project platform is password protected and the data collected are anonymized. To maintain students' anonymity and to comply with university research review conventions, no citations are attached to student quotes in this chapter, so that no identifying student information is given. Also, the age associated with student quotes is approximate. This is because students join the platform as a classroom: the classroom grade-level is known, but student age is approximated since there are a range of ages in a grade. The quotes in the chapter give information about students' approximate age rather than their grade-level because grade-level numbering varies across countries.

10 Horowitz, A. (2013). *On looking: Eleven Walks with Expert Eyes*. New York: Simon and Schuster.

11 Salopek, P. (2016, June 2). Watch: An ancient prairie comes back to life. Out of Eden Walk. *National Geographic*. Retrieved from http://www.nationalgeographic.org/projects/out-of-eden-walk/articles/2016-06-watch-an-ancient-prairie-comes-back-to-life

12 Horowitz, p. 186.

13 Honoré, C. (2004). In Praise of Slow: How a Worldwide Movement is Challenging the Cult of Speed. Toronto: Vintage Canada.

14 Honoré, C. (n.d.). *In Praise of Slow*. Retrieved from http://www.carlhonore.com/books/in-praise-of-slowness/.

15 Ibid.

16 See, for example, http://www.mindfulschools.org/.

CHAPTER 4

Looking and Describing

Slow looking and description are unavoidably linked, because when we take the time to observe things closely, we also usually describe them, either to others or to ourselves. We saw this happen with the students in the Out of Eden Learn program, and we can imagine it easily ourselves. Suppose I ask you to mentally compose a few sentences describing the page or screen on which you are reading these words. It might strike you as an odd request, but by the time you reach your third sentence, you will probably notice features you weren't initially aware of—the width of the margins, maybe, or the surface texture of the page. Moreover, because this is a book on slow looking, you might be primed to look for visual details in a way that you wouldn't be if it was a different kind of book. The process of composing a description propels our perceptions forward so that we literally see more things, and the mindset we bring to the experience shapes what we see.

This chapter looks at various ways that slow looking and description are connected. It begins, simply enough, with a definition. Description is the process of representing how something appears, in order to capture or communicate a vivid sense of what it's like. The word is derived from the Latin *describere*, which means to write things down. We typically associate description with linguistic expression, such as a journal entry, or a verbal recounting of an observation, but descriptions needn't be limited to words. For example, observational drawing is a form of description, because it involves pictorially representing how something appears. Music or sound can be descriptive when used to convey a vivid impression of an experience, such as a clap that describes the sound of thunder, or a musical piece that evokes a sense of a pastoral scene. Movement, too, can be a form of description—when someone uses her hands to describe a friend's height, for instance, or as a dancer unfolds his body to represent the sun rising.

To see how description works, let's begin with words. Consider this passage from the American novel *The Adventures of Huckleberry Finn*. Huck is watching the sun rise over the Mississippi River. See how his leisurely description shapes each perception as it unfolds.

> Not a sound anywhere—perfectly still—just like the whole world was asleep, only sometimes the bullfrogs a-cluttering, maybe. The first thing to see, looking away over the water, was a kind of dull line—that was the wood on t'other side; you couldn't make nothing else out; then a pale place in the sky; then more paleness spreading around; then the river softened up, away off, and warn't black anymore but gray; you could see little dark spots drifting along, ever so far away—trading scows, and such things . . .[1]

We can feel Huck's view of the scene expand and take shape as he draws out his words. This isn't just a literary technique: scientists and poets alike use the process of verbal description to bring their observations into finer focus, just as visual artists use the process of sketching in order to "see" what they see. In an important way, description is an engine of slow looking. It drives the process of observation forward because it provides structures to deepen one's looking. More than that, the methods and mental frames we bring to the act of description profoundly shape what we see. For example, in the passage above, we see the sunrise through Huck's eyes—and, because Huck is a fictional character, we see it through the author's eyes as well. If Huck was a different kind of character—say a Mississippi shipping merchant rather than a 14-year-old boy—he may have observed more detail in the little dark spots he passingly calls "trading scows, and such things." If the author, Samuel Clemens (better known as Mark Twain), hadn't spent time as a young man working as a Mississippi riverboat pilot, his character Huck might be less attuned to the way the river "softened up, away off" as the sky lightened at dawn.

Features of Description

We tend to use the word describe loosely. For instance, we talk about describing our thoughts, our feelings, or our sensory impressions. We might describe a bus trip we took, a meal we ate, or our views about the meaning of life. But when it comes to slow looking, description primarily relates to phenomena that are observable through the senses. Correspondingly, this chapter is about descriptions of such phenomena—that is, descriptions about things that you can see, hear, smell, feel, and taste. With this framing in mind, take a moment to ponder this question: What makes a description a description? You might find the question challenging to answer with words but easy to answer intuitively. You'd know a description when you see or hear one, and you'd know how to produce one when asked. For example, suppose I ask you to give me a description of the view outside your window. You'd immediately understand that I'm asking you to tell me about the various observable features of the scene—the objects you see, the shape of the landscape, the color of the buildings or sky, and so on. Without thinking much about it, you'd also understand that I'm not asking for a history of your neighborhood, or an analysis of the politics of your neighbors, or a lengthy discourse on the state of neighborliness in the world today. Rather, my request is perfectly straightforward—I'm simply asking for a description that will help me picture for myself what you see and sense.

Description as a "Cognitive Frame"

The scholar Werner Wolf talks about description as a "cognitive frame."[2] By this he means that when we engage in the act of description—and also when we read, hear, or otherwise receive descriptions composed by others—we are mentally attuned to certain kinds of knowable features. Specifically, we're alert to how things appear. As Wolf explains, descriptions aim to communicate the "whatness" of things—what objects and phenomena seem to be like on their surface, rather than why they exist or how they work or the function they serve. The reason you so readily know what I'm asking for when I ask you to describe the view from your window is because you intuitively take on this cognitive frame: you know that I'm interested in the "whatness" of what you see.

One way to bring the concept of description into relief is to look at how it compares to other cognitive frames. In literature, for example, description contrasts with narrative. A descriptive passage in a literary work—whether a novel, a short story, an essay, or a poem—conveys a sense of how something appears at a particular moment in time, whereas a narrative passage tells the story of things happening over a period of time. Another way to put this is that description is topographical; it describes perceptible features. Narrative is temporal; it concerns the relationship of the past, present, and future.

Of course, most works of literature braid description and narrative together, and the distinction between them is not a sharp line, but rather a matter of emphasis. Think back to the passage from *Huckleberry Finn*. As Huck describes the sunrise over the Mississippi River, time is certainly passing—specifically, the time it takes for the sun to rise. But the emphasis of the passage is descriptive; it foregrounds a sense of presentness as Huck relays his impressions. Though the scene unfolds over several moments, we have no trouble holding it steady in our mind's eye in order to picture it.

Even scenes that unfold over years can have this sense of presentness. Here is nature writer Barry Lopez describing the migration of caribou in his book *Arctic Dreams*:

> After the herds have gone, the calving grounds can seem like the most deserted places on earth, even if you can sense strongly that the caribou will be back next year. When they do return, hardly anything will have changed. A pile of caribou droppings may take thirty years to remineralize on the calving grounds. The carcass of a wolf-killed caribou may lie undisturbed for three or four years. Time pools in the stillness here and then dissipates. The country is emptied of movement.[3]

This presentness is an important quality of descriptions. Wolf points out that descriptions tend not to evoke a sense of suspense, which is partly how they function as a cognitive frame. We don't expect descriptions to keep us on the edge of our seats, waiting to hear what happens next; rather, we expect them to evoke a vivid sense of things as they appear, bracketed in a moment—even a prolonged moment—so that they conjure up an image or sensory impression.

The descriptive and narrative frames contrast in the visual arts as well. Although the visual arts tend to use the term "depiction" instead of "description", it amounts to the same thing, which is to convey a vivid sense of appearance. Superficially, painting and sculpture seem to be especially descriptive in spirit, in large part because these art forms are static, and thus seem to be "about" how things appear at the moment. But of course paintings and sculptures also tell stories—many stories. For example, a painting of a battlefield tells the story of a historical event. It also tells a story of a cultural mindset, as well as a biographical story about the artist and her time; perhaps also a story about the creative process as seen through the various choices the artist makes. By contrast, the depictive dimension of a sculpture has more to do with how particular parts of the work are rendered so as to vividly convey the surface appearance of objects or events. The depiction might be the lace of a collar, the swell of an ocean wave, the straining tendons in a horse's neck. As with verbal description, the purpose of pictorial "whatness" is to be evocative. Its aim is to conjure up a vivid sensory impression of the thing it depicts. Artists have many different ways of evoking these vivid impressions—it's part of the artistry of art: the spare, graceful lines of Matisse's figures are as descriptive of the human form as Leonardo da Vinci's intense and beautifully detailed drawings.

In science, the cognitive frame that contrasts with description is different. Instead of being narrative, it is explanatory. Scientists sometimes distinguish between descriptive research, which has to do with observing, recording and classifying natural phenomena without a specific research question in mind, and hypothesis-driven research, which focuses on producing explanations of how something works, often through experimentation. This is a broad characterization, and again the line can blur: virtually all scientists are concerned with explanation at some level of their work, just as all scientists must base their work in objectively observable (i.e. "descriptive") data. But clearly some scientific endeavors have a special focus on the "whatness" of things, while others focus on the how and why. For example, a marine biologist's work might have a more descriptive flavor when she is exploring an uncharted region of the ocean floor, and a more explanatory flavor later on when she is examining the effects of ocean temperatures on the fish population in that region. And while description and explanation interweave closely in scientific practice, each frame has its own moves and standards. Description involves observing and recording details perceived either through the senses directly or with the aid of instrumentation. Moreover, the described phenomena must be observable by others, at least in theory. Explanation involves seeking causes, drawing inferences, forming and testing hypotheses, and making predictions.

What does all of this have to do with slow looking? Like description, slow looking involves a cognitive frame that focuses on the whatness of things. It foregrounds noticing how things are, rather than telling a story about why they are the way they are, or how they came to be.

Description and Detail

> I own a creaky old wooden office chair that swivels, tilts, and rolls. . . . It's a so-called banker's chair, with a scooped seat, curved arms, and a contoured back . . ."[4]
>
> (Witold Rybczynski)

In addition to being a distinctive cognitive frame, descriptions tend to have some degree of detail. If you ask me to describe the object I'm sitting on and I simply say "chair," you probably won't be satisfied. You'd want at least a little more information—such as what style the chair is, what material it's made of, whether, like Rybczynski's chair, it "swivels, tilts, and rolls." In order for a description to fulfill its function of evoking a vivid impression, it usually needs to go beyond a one-word identifier. There are a variety of ways to make this happen: features can be enumerated, comparisons can be made, essential characteristics can be emphasized, key qualities can be distilled. Here is another description of sunrise, this time from the novel *Fingersmith* by Sarah Waters. Like Huck's sunrise, there are smudges of industry on the horizon, but the feel is very different.

> *The morning has broken.*—I thought of the morning like an egg, that had split with a crack and was spreading. Before us lay all the green country of England, with its rivers and its roads and its hedges, its churches, its chimneys, its rising threads of smoke. The chimneys grew taller, the roads and rivers wider, the threads of smoke more thick, the farther off the country spread; until at last, at the farthest point of all, they made a smudge, a stain, a darkness—a darkness, like the darkness of the coal in a fire—a darkness that was broken, here and there, where the sun caught panes of glass and the golden tips of domes and steeples, with glittering points of light.
>
> 'London,' I said. 'Oh, London!'[5]

Sometimes evocativeness is achieved by giving ample detail, as in Waters' description of London. But it can also be achieved through concentrated spareness. Haiku is a form of poetry that is decidedly descriptive because it's about capturing the immediate sense of something. But a haiku only consists of three brief lines. Its length is sometimes described as the time it takes to draw a single breath, and its evocativeness comes from the artful juxtaposition of a just a small number of elements.

> A summer river being crossed
> How pleasing
> With my sandals in my hand
> (Yosa Buson, eighteenth century)

The spare details of this poem coalesce perfectly to evoke a vivid sensory impression: I can hear the rush of the river, feel it flowing over my bare feet and ankles, smell the crispness of the air (I picture it as a mountain river), even if these details aren't explicitly named.

Description and the Subject/Object Distinction

Another characteristic of description has to do with the sense of distance, or separation, between the observer and the object described. To describe something involves making a subject/object distinction. To have the vantage point of an observer, we imagine at least some part of ourselves outside of the thing observed.

Legions of semioticians and philosophers have thought deeply about thorny puzzles concerning the human sense of the subject/object distinction, pondering how we acquire it, what it signifies, and whether such a distinction is even logically tenable given the built-in limitations of the human mind. With much respect, I tiptoe at the edges of this vast body of work, and make the simple point that our intuitive understanding of the concept of description includes a sense that there is some measure of separation between the describer and the described; otherwise our sense of self would flow into everything around us and we wouldn't have any feeling of demarcation between ourselves and other things. To get a feel for what I mean, return to the scene outside your window that I asked you to describe. No matter how subjectively you are entangled with what you see, when I asked for a description, you probably immediately put a certain cognitive distance between the scene and yourself. In other words, you conceptualized the scene as knowable outside your own mind and body. This doesn't necessarily mean that you took an objectivist stance. There are many flavors of distance between the describer and the described, both across and within disciplinary perspectives. One naturalist might take a cool and dry approach to describing her field observations; another might adopt a livelier, involved stance. Some journalists report in a hard-news objectivist style, others—like Paul Salopek—are embedded in the stories they write about and make their experience part of the story.

In a moment we turn to some specific strategies for creating descriptions. But first a quick summary so far. The foregoing sections have discussed three aspects of our common understanding of description. First, we understand description as a cognitive frame that orients our attention to the surface features of things. It contrasts with a narrative cognitive frame that emphasizes storytelling, and with an explanatory cognitive frame that emphasizes analysis and interpretation. Second, we understand that descriptions go beyond mere naming: to describe something means to give a representation of it that is sufficiently vivid to conjure up an impression of the thing described. Finally, we understand that the act of description involves making a subject/object mental move: to describe something is to assume, at least for the moment, a separation between the observer and the thing described.

Description and slow looking are frequently connected because they support one another. In the process of looking slowly at something, it helps to describe what we see; when we are composing a description, it helps to slow down to look more closely. But though the two are often linked, they needn't be. For instance, description involves some sort of representation or recounting of what one sees; however, there are mindful and meditative versions of slow looking that emphasize being alert to the flow of sense impressions as they wash over us without making a conscious effort to articulate or "re-present" them. Similarly, slow looking involves going beyond a quick glance, and there are descriptive techniques that intentionally aim to capture the feeling of *not* going beyond a quick glance. For example, what's sometimes called stream of consciousness or impressionistic writing aims to capture a rapid, unreflective flow of immediate sense impressions and feelings. But even these outlying examples share a cognitive frame with slow looking—a mindset that emphasizes "whatness" over how-ness, why-ness or wherefore-ness. So, to understand how description works is to understand an important dimension of slow looking.

SLOW LOOKING AND STRATEGIES FOR DESCRIPTION

People who study how the mind works—philosophers as well as scientists —might argue that any kind of conscious mental picturing of things involves description, because we can't avoid using cognitive frames to shape our ideas. In other words, mindfulness practices and stream-of-consciousness writing notwithstanding, we describe our sense impressions to ourselves because there's no other way for us to be conscious of them. Technically this may be true, but from the standpoint of everyday experience, we immediately understand the difference between intentionally composing a description and just "having" a sense impression. To see what I mean, try this: look around you and notice an object nearby. Quickly tell yourself what it is, and then avert your eyes. Now, look at the same object again and take a few minutes to mentally describe it, as if you are telling someone what it looks like. If you take some time with this exercise, you might notice that the act of composing the description helps you maintain attentional focus and increases your powers of observation. As you begin to describe things you will almost certainly notice more than you thought you saw on first impression.

Look for Detail

The idea that description encourages close looking is familiar to anyone who teaches writing: set students the task of writing a detailed description of an object or scene, and in the process they will record many more aspects of it than they saw at first glance. So from an educational standpoint, one of the simplest ways to teach slow looking is to give students time and encouragement to describe in writing what they see. We saw this broad strategy at work in the Out of Eden Learn program discussed in the previous chapter. The program gave students ample time to use pictures and words to describe the ordinary scenes of their daily lives. The process of crafting these descriptions and sharing them with their fellow students worked exactly as it was supposed to: it encouraged students to slow down and notice the details of their surroundings.

Noticing is key to one of the most common descriptive approaches: the giving of ample detail. A beautiful example comes from the work of photographer and naturalist David Liittschwager. In a blend of science and art, his *One Cubic Foot* project involves inserting the open frame of a cubic foot into a variety of natural environments, from Central Park in New York to Table Mountain in South Africa. (Full-color versions of Liittschwager's photographs can be found online.)

At each installation he works with several collaborators to describe and photograph in detail every living creature that lives in or moves through the framed space over the course of 24 hours. Here is an excerpt from one of Liittschwager's early collaborators, the biologist E. O. Wilson, describing what he sees in a cube:

> There are the insect myriads creeping and buzzing among the weeds, the worms and unnameable creatures that squirm or scuttle for cover when you turn garden soil for planting. There are those annoying ants that swarm out when their nest is accidentally cut open and the pesky beetle grubs exposed at yellowed grass roots. When you flip a rock over, there are even more: you see spiderlings and sundry pale unknowns of diverse form slinking through mats of fungus strands. Tiny beetles hide from the sudden light, and pill bugs curl their bodies into defensive balls. Centipedes and millipedes, the armored snakes of their size class, squeeze into the nearest crevices and wormholes.[6]

Wilson's description is reminiscent of *inventorying*, the broad cross-disciplinary observation strategy that was discussed in Chapter 2. But Wilson does

Figure 4.1 Table Mountain, Cape Town, South Africa.
© David Liittschwager, from his *One Cubic Foot* series. Photo courtesy of the artist.

more than merely make a list: his vivid description—the creeping, buzzing, scuttling, squirming movement of the bugs—uses an abundance of detail to bring the description to life.

Elaborating upon detail is almost synonymous with our everyday idea of description, and strategies and advice about how to do it abound. Teachers of writing tell their students to notice with all their senses (what do you see, hear, touch, taste?), to elaborate on what they see, to see in slow motion, to provide more detail. The core move behind all these strategies is to look for *more*—more features, more particularities, more nuance, more detail.

Look from Different Vantage Points

In addition to looking for detail, a second and complementary strategy for encouraging description is to look from different vantage points. This approach has to do with switching up one's point of view in order to see things in a new way. There are three broad types of vantage-point strategies, each of which is a familiar mainstay of descriptive practice.

Physical Vantage Point

This has to do with altering one's physical perspective in order to see and describe things from a different angle. This theme is already familiar: in Chapter 2 we looked at how the *scale and scope* observation strategy emphasizes looking at things from the vantage point of different physical perspectives—far away or close up, above or below. Relatedly, in the last chapter we saw how students in the Out of Eden Learn program take photographs from unusual physical perspectives—a bug's view of a tree, a cityscape reflected in a puddle—and often use their photos as inspiration for extensive verbal description.

A classic and still stunning example of vantage-point description is the 1977 short film called *Powers of Ten*, produced by designers Charles and Ray Eames.[7] The film begins with an aerial shot of two people having a picnic in a park in Chicago. The first shot is taken from a metre above the couple, and every 10 seconds the shot zooms up ten times the previous distance, first to 10 metres above, then a hundred, then a thousand, and so on. At each vantage point, the narrator briefly describes the view. We see the whole of the lakeside park, then the shoreline of Chicago, then a few leaps later, the blue marble of the earth, and then the whole of the solar system. A few more leaps hurtle us through the Milky Way and out of the galaxy until eventually we are 100 million light years away from earth. From this vantage point the view is mainly dark, with only the tiniest flecks of distant light. The narrator describes: "This lonely scene, the galaxies like dust, is what most of space looks like." At this point the camera reverses its journey and telescopes rapidly back to earth until it reaches the hand of the man sleeping on the picnic blanket. Here it slows again to its power-of-ten pace to zoom into the man's skin, reducing the distance by 90 per cent every 10 seconds. The narrator resumes his description of vantage points: first we travel through layers of skin into a blood vessel; through outer layers of cells and "felty collagen," into a white blood cell, then through the "coiled coils of DNA" until eventually we reach the vibrating nucleus of a single carbon atom. The entire film is 9 minutes long.

Making the Familiar Strange

The dazzling and sometimes dizzying vantage points we experience in *Powers of Ten* point to another broad type of vantage-point strategy: making the familiar strange.

Suppose you are a four-footed creature contentedly living in the forest. One day you come across a most unusual object—a leather pouchlike container, the size and shape of a hollowed-out squirrel minus its tail, with crisscrossed vines threaded through holes on its top. You sniff it warily—it smells of large animal. Later you learn that it is called a human shoe.

Looking at something from a vantage point that defamiliarizes it is a common descriptive strategy. Similar to what the Out of Eden Learn students called *seeing with fresh eyes*, it works by shaking up what we take for granted so that we see things in a new light. The strategy is part of the toolkit of anthropologists and sociologists, who often try to defamiliarize themselves with their own cultural assumptions in order to describe human behavior and culture from a fresh perspective. For example, a cultural anthropologist might choose to look at the spiky metal object next to her dinner plate not as a fork, but as an unfamiliar artifact that offers a window into the customs and conventions of a distant tribe. This mental move, of intentionally distancing oneself from everyday assumptions, is also a common element of strategies meant to encourage creative problem solving and innovation. The basic idea is to describe a problem from an unfamiliar vantage point in order to explore novel solutions. One such approach is Synectics, a creative problem solving approach that emphasizes analogy-making as a route to creative insight.[8] The technique involves making the familiar very, very strange by intentionally reaching for highly unusual comparisons to spark ideas. For example, suppose you are trying to design a pair of folding eyeglasses that can fit inside a wallet. Instead of viewing it as a problem of hinges, try comparing the problem to, say, a spider trying to scuttle under a door. Or if that doesn't work, compare it to the knee joints of a moose walking through snow. Or if that doesn't work . . . well, you get the idea.

Take on Different Personas

The third vantage-point strategy for description may be the most familiar: it is the strategy of describing things from the vantage point of a persona other than your own. Young children do it when they play make believe; artists and writers do it when they create characters; all of us do it when we try to envision or empathize with the lives of other people. In the broadest sense, fiction is defined by the taking on of personas, because it is about telling stories from the point of view of imagined characters. It becomes a descriptive strategy when the persona describes the "whatness" of the world it encounters. Usually the persona vantage point is human, but it needn't be. Franz Kafka's novel *Metamorphosis* is told from the perspective of Gregor, a young man who wakes up one day to find himself turned into a giant cockroach.[9] Kafka's description of Gregor's life through this vantage point not only communicates the incredible horror and inconvenience of having the body of a giant insect in a world built for humans—an echo of the "making the familiar strange" strategy discussed above—but also captures the feelings of alienation and isolation experienced by the radical outsider.

The strategy of taking on unusual non-human personas isn't limited to animate creatures. In an entirely different spirit, the children's story *I, Doko: The Tale of a Basket* describes the life of a family in a Nepalese village through the perspective of a large basket.[10] The basket recounts how it carries the family's babies, its bundles, and ultimately its infirmed elders. The descriptions of family life the basket shares from its unique perspective are both poignant and surprising.

The examples of a Nepalese basket and a giant insect a notwithstanding, by far the most common persona people take on is the perspective of another human being. The idioms we have for this strategy are familiar: put yourself in someone else's shoes; see the world through someone else's eyes. We proffer this advice readily, and in many schools it's a staple of educational fare. In language arts classes students read and write stories from other people's perspectives; in history classes they explore the past through the lenses of historical figures; in schools with robust art programs students experiment with taking on others' personas through theater and dance.

The inclination to try to see the world through the perspective of other people is so common that we accept it almost unthinkingly. But it is worth pointing out that while it is the most natural and important of human capacities, it is also the most frightening. It is natural because it is a normal and necessary stage of child development: at a very young age, children learn that other people may see the world differently than they do and that it is useful to be able to envision what they see. The black lines a child paints on her face are meant to be cat's whiskers, but by three years old she already knows that her mother will likely see things differently and make her wash them off. From a humanistic and social standpoint, the capacity to see the world from other people's perspectives is one of the most important human achievements, because it allows us to envision and care about the needs and concerns of others. But the ease with which we can imagine another's point of view is also frightening, because of how quickly it can lead to harmful ideas and actions. To step into someone else's shoes involves the feeling that one has some knowledge about those shoes. But that knowledge is always incomplete, often overly simplistic, and sometimes dangerously wrong. Moreover, even if some of what we think we know is accurate, it is always only part of the picture: we can never fully inhabit the lived experiences of other people. The paradox of perspective-taking is that on the one hand, it is disrespectful of the integrity of another person's experience to assume that we can know it, particularly when the experience is so distant from our own that we almost certainly risk resorting to stereotypes in order to imagine it. On the other hand, without the capacity to imagine experience from another's point of view, humankind is lost. The moral value of perspective taking may be second only to our capacity to understand its limits.

So far, this discussion of the limitations of perspective-taking ignores the limitations of the most common perspective of all: our own. The three broad descriptive strategies just discussed—looking for detail, making the familiar strange, and looking from different vantage points—are all strategies that we can intentionally decide whether or not to pursue. But we can't decide not to be ourselves. And even the most ordinary act of description reflects the vantage point of the expectations, biases and background assumptions that each of us bring to our everyday encounters. If I describe to you some people I saw in the supermarket this morning, it will not be a neutral description: without my intending to, I will have noticed and described certain of their features and not others. For instance, I may not have noticed certain details of their appearance or behavior because they were a lot like mine—or maybe I *did* notice these things because they weren't like mine. Our ingrained selectivity doesn't mean that we can't change or improve the way we naturally view things. There is much we can and should do to learn about our own biases, and appreciate the limits of our own knowledge. But we can't *not* have a subjective vantage point. The unavoidable selectivity of the human eye—and heart—is relevant not just to the process of description, but to the entire theme of slow looking. This theme is picked up again in Chapter 8, which focuses on how slow looking is a way of learning about various sorts of complexity in the world, including the complexity of our own involvement in the act of looking.

More than Words

Most of the examples in the foregoing sections have characterized description primarily as a written or verbal activity—something that unfolds through words. But words are only one of the body's languages. Just as we observe the world through many senses, we can describe it through many modalities as well—through sound, through gesture, and perhaps most notably, through the making of marks.

"Drawing," says art scholar John Berger, "is a form of probing."[11] His comment points to the fact that the process of describing what one sees— in the case of drawing, through the medium of line rather than words— functions as an act of discovery as much as an act of description. To make a drawing is to look with the hand as well as the eye. Drawing is a physical act, and sometimes the hand leads the way. "When I make my drawings," said the artist Alberto Giacometti, "the path traced by my pencil on the sheet of paper is, to some extent, analogous to the gesture of a man groping his way in the darkness."

My sister is an artist. She mainly paints, but she often sketches in preparation for a painting, and she talks about how sketching helps her to see beyond the objects at the center of her attentional focus so that she discovers the shapes that surround them—the space between the rungs of a chair, for example, or the open oval between the handles of a pair of pliers. A classic drawing exercise that vividly brings this out is contour drawing, a technique whereby one creates a visual description by drawing a continuous line that captures all the visible contours of an object or scene. An even more concentrated version of the exercise, sometime called blind contour drawing, involves tracing the contours of scene or object without looking at the paper, keeping one's eyes fastened firmly on the object of observation so that one's whole focus is on visual discovery rather than on creating a pleasing picture. Try it: either version of contour drawing is a great way to experience the connection between drawing and slow looking.

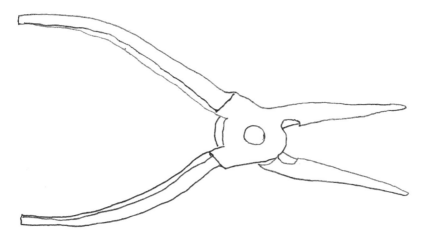

Figure 4.2
Drawing by Andrea Tishman.

Scientists, too, use drawing as a form of slow looking. In an essay entitled *Why Sketch*, science illustrator Jenny Keller puts it like this:

> Drawing makes you look more carefully at your subject. As an observational tool, drawing requires that you pay attention to every detail—even the seemingly unimportant ones. In creating an image (no matter how skillfully), the lines and tones on the paper provide ongoing feedback as to what you have observed closely and what you have not. If, for example, up to a certain point you have ignored the toes of your mammal, a quick glance at the toeless creature on the page will direct your attention to precisely that neglected feature. Just the act of making the drawing will force you to examine each and every part of your subject.[12]

Keller's essay is one of several in a wonderful compendium of essays by scientists called *Field Notes on Science & Nature*, edited by Michael Canfield. Not all scientists include sketches in their field notes, but many do, and one can see in the diversity of their drawings the wide range of styles and purposes of sketching as part of scientific observation. Jenny Keller makes beautiful watercolors of coral and jellyfish that show a long, lingering attention to detail. The quick, expressive sketches by Zoologist Jonathan Kingdon show the dynamism of observation as he captures the vitality of the head movements of a *caracal*—a wild African cat.

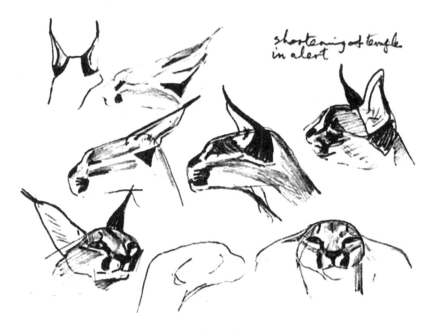

Figure 4.3 Jonathan Kingdon's Caracal cat drawings.
Michael Canfield's *Field Notes on Science and Nature*, Reproduced with permission of the artist. Image courtesy of Harvard University Press.

From a description of a sunrise over the Mississippi to the drawings of an African cat, the throughline of this chapter has been how the descriptive process provides a structure that allows slow looking to unfold. Huck Finn gazes out at the river and widens the scope of his perceptions as he leisurely describes them. Jonathan Kingdon discovers new features of the caracal's head movements as he writes and sketches in his field notebook. My sister makes a drawing of an everyday tool and discovers the shapes hidden in its interstices. From the standpoint of education, the relationship between description and slow looking offers rich instructional opportunities. Writing exercises can encourage students to look slowly by asking them to describe what they see from various vantage points; drawing activities can encourage students to slow down and literally see with their hands. Though this chapter mainly focuses on words and pictures, other languages of the body also offer opportunities. I remember watching a kindergarten teacher show a vibrant abstract painting to her students. First she asked them to choose a line or shape in the picture and make the shape with their bodies. Then she instructed them to move their bodies in the way they thought the shape might move in the picture. The classroom erupted into a joyous, wriggling mass of bodies as the children zigged and zagged across the room. Afterwards, the teacher directed students' attention back to the picture and asked them to talk about what they saw in it. I was amazed by the vividness of their observations.

At the heart of all the descriptive activities discussed in this chapter is the assumption that the person doing the describing—a real-life person or a fictional character—is looking at the target of the description for him or herself. The kindergarteners are looking at the painting directly, rather than listening to the teacher describe it to them. Scientists make field notes as a result of actually being in the field, not just reading other observers' accounts. The Nepalese basket has a front row seat from which to directly observe three generations of family. This point, about the centrality of direct observation, may seem so obvious that it's not worth mentioning. But actually, much of education is about learning about what other people describe—usually experts—rather than looking for oneself. Imagine a child engrossed in observing a starfish. She could surely pick up a book and see pictures or read descriptions of it produced by far more expert observers. But you'd probably have to pry her away from the starfish to get her to do so. From the standpoint of learning, there is something singularly powerful about looking for oneself. Which raises the very interesting question of why direct observation is such a compelling and engaging learning behavior. The next chapter begins by turning to this question.

Notes

1   For an online reprint of *The Adventures of Huckleberry Finn* by Mark Twain, see http://www.gutenberg.org/files/76/76-h/76-h.htm#contents. The selection is from the opening paragraph in Chapter 19.

2   Wolf, W. (2007). Description as a transmedial mode of representation: General feature and possibilities of realization in painting, fiction, and music. In W. Wolf & W. Bernhart (Eds.), *Description in Literature and Other Media* (1–87). Amsterdam: Rodopi.

3   Lopez, B. (2001). *Arctic Dreams*. New York: First Vintage Books, pp. 170–171.

4   Rybczynski, W. (2016). *Now I Sit Me Down: From Klismos to Plastic Chair: A Natural History*. New York: Farrar, Straus and Giroux, p. 3.

5   Waters, S. (2002). *Fingersmith*. New York: Riverhead Books, p. 496.

6   Wilson, E. O & Liittschwager, D. (2010, Feb.). *National Geographic*. Retrieved from http://ngm.nationalgeographic.com/2010/02/cubic-foot/wilson-text. Reprinted with permission from Edward O. Wilson.

7   Office of Charles and Ray Eames. (1977). *Powers of ten*. Retrieved from https://www.youtube.com/watch?v=0fKBhvDjuy0.

8   Gordon, W. J. J. (1961). *Synectics: The Development of Creative Capacity*. New York: Harper & Row.
9   Kafka, F. (1988). The Metamorphosis, In The Penal Colony, and Other Stories. New York: Schocken Books.
10 Young, E. (2004). *I, Doko: The Tale of a Basket*. New York: Philomel Books.
11 Berger, J. (2011). *Bento's Sketchbook*. New York: Pantheon Books, p. 150.
12 Canfield, M. R. (Ed.). (2011). *Field Notes on Science & Nature*. Cambridge: Harvard University Press, pp. 161–162.

CHAPTER 5

Look for Yourself . . . and Visit a Museum

Imagine it's a beautiful day and you're walking along a beach with a friend. An incoming wave rolls ashore, and as it recedes it deposits a glistening seashell in its wake. Your friend bends down to pick it up. "How interesting!" she says as she examines it. "I've never seen a shell like this." Intrigued, you lean in to look, ignoring the fleeting impulse to pluck the shell from her hands to get a better view. "Here," she says after a moment, handing it to you, "take a look."

This impulse, to get a good look for oneself, is so familiar that we hardly notice it. Whether it's an object in nature or a work of art or a commotion on the sidewalk, when something sparks our curiosity, we tend to want to look at it with our own eyes. Of course, it's not always practical to look for oneself. It can be too costly, time consuming, or dependent on specialized skill and training. Wildlife biologists might travel the globe to observe animals in their natural habitats. Most of us will simply visit the zoo. Still, there are plenty of everyday situations like the one with the seashell, in which the impulse to look for oneself can be satisfied with relatively little effort—all one needs to do is take a look. But even when the route to satisfaction seems straightforward, there are some interesting ways it can be thwarted.

For example, suppose that instead of showing you the shell, your friend kept it cupped in her hands and began describing its features to you in elaborate detail. Chances are you'd find this quite unsatisfying, even if you could perfectly envision the shell as she described it. Or suppose that instead of showing you the shell, your friend casually threw it back into the waves. No big deal, perhaps, but as she tossed it out of reach you'd likely feel at least a momentary pinch of thwarted curiosity. Or suppose that your friend, an avid seashell collector, used her phone to Google the shell and immediately determined its genus and species. You might be curious about what she found out, but it wouldn't do as a substitute: you'd still want to look at the shell for yourself.

Of course, these things are unlikely to happen. Like most people, your friend instinctively appreciates the desire to look for oneself, and she kindly hands you the shell. You examine it for a moment, turning it over in your hands, and notice a few of its striking features—the colored striations on the outer shell, its glossy enamel-like interior. Your curiosity satisfied, you hand the shell back to your friend. She tucks it in her pocket, and the two of you resume your walk.

The impulse to look at things for ourselves is irrepressible and ubiquitous. Think of how many times a day you pause to observe something that catches your eye. There's a reason for this, and it's more than simply to satisfy a passing spark of curiosity. When we look at things for ourselves, we take in a huge amount of integrated information. Consider the seashell. If you spent just 5 seconds looking at it and holding it in your hand, you'd likely notice its shape, its colors, and its textures inside and out. You may also notice clues about its age (multiple concentric ridges, for example) and about its former inhabitant (perhaps through the remnants of a fibrous muscle). Moreover, you'd connect it to *you*. You'd know if you had seen this kind of shell before, whether it's an object of interest to you, and whether it connects to other things you know about. All this in much less time than it takes to read these words.

The Many Outcomes of Looking for Oneself

Looking for oneself is a knowledge-seeking behavior prompted by a spectrum of reasons. At one end of the spectrum are instinctive acts of looking that are automatic reactions to stimuli. We hear a loud noise behind us and we turn to look. At this end of the spectrum, the impulse to look for oneself is common to most sentient creatures, and its function is to provide information related to survival. It tells an organism whether there's a predator or other imminent threat in the vicinity, whether it needs to fight or flee, whether food is nearby, whether there is a reproductive opportunity available. The act of looking—or of smelling, touching, or any other way of quickly gathering information through the senses—is triggered by instinct, not by conscious intent.

At the other end of the spectrum are acts of looking driven by curiosity or interest, and the reasons behind them are more varied. For example, we look in order to confirm or deny the reality of something, such as when we look out of the window to confirm whether it's raining. We look for ourselves in order to get a holistic picture of something or a quick read of a situation, such as when we glance into a restaurant to see if it's the kind of place we'd like to eat. We look for ourselves to see if we can imagine things differently, for example when we study the layout of furniture in a room and envision moving things around. We look for ourselves in order to experience the complicated shock of seeing something gruesome or the thrill of viewing something freakish, such as when we crane our necks to see a car accident or marvel at the performance of a contortionist. We look for ourselves in order to experience the guilty pleasure of beholding the forbidden, such as when we peek behind closed doors. We look for ourselves simply to see what's there, such as when we take a tour of a new city or glance in a shop window or look at a seashell our friend happened to pick up.

The reasons that motivate direct observation are varied, but the common thread across them is that the act of looking for oneself is cognitive. It is directed toward learning or perceiving something new. Moreover, looking for oneself is often a form of concentrated cognition, because even a quick glance—like looking at the seashell—enables us to learn several different kinds of things at once.

It is noteworthy that as one moves away from the survival side of the spectrum, the act of looking is often a pleasurable affair. Its pleasures are variable and complicated, from the simple itch-scratching pleasure of gratifying one's curiosity to the complex satisfaction of spending an hour looking at a work of art. Of course, there are many unpleasant and painful things we look at for ourselves, too. But whether the impulse to look for oneself is driven by interest, curiosity, pleasure-seeking, or just plain survival, the power of our desire to look at things for ourselves is persistent and deep. So much so that humankind has a long and robust history of cultural institutions devoted to it.

The Earliest Museum?

In 1925, the archaeologist Leonard Woolley made an unusual discovery. He and his team were excavating a palace in the ancient Sumerian city of Ur. As they were digging in one of the large internal chambers of the palace, they uncovered a group of artifacts that at first seemed to make no sense: fragments of statues and stones from a variety of time periods that seemed carefully arranged. All of the artifacts were older than the site of the palace, and some predated it by almost 1,500 years. Moreover, many of the fragments had edges that appeared to have been smoothed, as if prepared for display. Continuing to dig, Woolley eventually uncovered several small clay cylinders with writing on them that described some of the artifacts in three languages. It didn't take long for him to realize that the cylinders were an ancient version of what museum professionals would call museum text or object labels.

Woolley's discovery has been called the world's first museum, and we now know that this proto-museum was the work of Princess Ennigaldi, daughter of Nabonidus, the last king of Babylon. Nabonidus was known to be intensely interested in the study of history, and perhaps especially interested in a version of history that justified his claim to the throne, since he acquired his kingship through warfare rather than ancestral lineage. As a princess, Ennigaldi's duties were to oversee the religious and educational life of the kingdom. The array of objects found in her chambers —many of which were previously excavated by Nabonidus himself— seemed to be organized to invite viewers to look at them closely and directly. We can't know exactly what the Princess hoped for in displaying the artifacts. Perhaps she hoped to inspire in viewers a sense of historical connectedness. Perhaps she wanted viewers to be awed by her family's erudition, or persuaded of the family's historical claim to the throne. Perhaps she thought the objects beautiful or wondrous and wished others to experience the pleasure of viewing them. Perhaps all of the above. What we do know is that the Princess's chamber, with its curated display of artifacts, closely resembles what our contemporary eyes would easily recognize as a museum.

The Idea of The Museum

Museums are cultural institutions devoted to the pleasure and power of looking at things for ourselves. Which is not to say that direct observation is their sole purpose; museums do many things, including collect, curate, preserve, restore, display, and archive objects and experiences, not to mention serve cultural and social spaces for civic gatherings. But if we didn't believe that allowing people to look at or otherwise directly experience things for themselves is a worthwhile pursuit, then instead of museums we'd have only warehouses and private collections.

It is hard to know exactly how many museums there are in the world, but a recent estimate puts the number at 55,000 in 202 countries.[1] This is a seriously large number. Anyone familiar with museums will know that the number includes a huge range of kinds of museums, from art museums to science museums, historic houses to botanical gardens and zoos, and even specialist museums like the museum of shovels or clocks or plumbing.

The fact that so many different kinds of museums exist says something important about the idea of the museum—how vividly it captures the public imagination and how well it serves as a center of gravity for a range of very different enterprises.

In her book *Museums in Motion*, Mary Alexander opens with this quote from museum educator Richard Grove:

> A hospital is a hospital. A library is a library. A rose is a rose. But a museum is Colonial Williamsburg, Mrs. Wilkerson's Figure Bottle Museum, the Museum of Modern Art, the Sea Lion Caves, the American Museum of Natural History, the Barton Museum of Whiskey History, The Cloisters, and Noell's Ark and Chimpanzee Farm and Gorilla Show.[2]

Grove was writing in 1969. Almost 50 years later, we could add an explosion of experiential museums to this list—from children's museums to science museums to news museums—and a huge range of online museums—from digital exhibitions of brick and mortar collections to museums that exist entirely online such as the gallery of Asian pop record covers and the museum of manhole covers. Indeed, there is even a Museum of Online Museums (MoOM), which collects and curates a vast array of online museum offerings. (The number of museums quoted above—55,000—does not include online museums, which are probably uncountable and ever-expanding.) Not only do museums vary widely in their offerings; they also vary in their purposes. Museums may communicate ideas about cultural value, stimulate curiosity, provide family-friendly leisure-time activities, or act as a nexus for social change and cultural exchange.

In fact, though many and probably most museums still center on a collection, over the past several decades museums have shifted somewhat away from an emphasis on "collect-and-preserve" and toward an emphasis on audience. As museum scholar Stephen Weil famously wrote on the cusp of the twenty-first century, museums are transitioning "from being *about* something to being *for* someone."[3] In the United States, this shift can be traced to what's often termed the Progressive Era, a period of social activism and political reform from roughly 1880–1920 that aimed to stop political corruption and improve the lives of individuals by countering the ill effects of urban-industrial civilization. Examining this history in his admirable book *Progressive Museum Practice*, scholar George Hein argues that the modern progressive idea of the museum—born in the spirit of the Progressive Era—is to contribute to the public good. Hein sees the museum as a socially progressive institution that offers visitors a range of educative and social experiences that can improve their lives and contribute to their capacity for democratic citizenry. This vision is at least partially realized today, as museums increasingly offer a range of activities, such as classes, lectures, film, theater, community convenings, social events, and family functions. Still, for an institution to label itself a museum, it must include somewhere in its makeup the possibility for visitors to have a direct experience with something—an experience that is not wholly didactic and which allows room for visitors to follow their own curiosity and make their own sense or meaning.

Museums and Concentrated Cognition

Given the stunning diversity of types of museums, and the wide range of activities that can take place within them, how is it that the idea of the museum holds together so well? Part of the answer has to do with the point made earlier in this chapter about the many purposes and outcomes of looking for oneself. We look for many reasons: To be persuaded of the truth of something; to "see with our own eyes"; to discern nuance and detail; to experience aesthetic pleasure; to gain information; to be horrified, thrilled, impressed, or delighted. Museums have a way of serving multiple purposes simultaneously without getting mired in the details. The fact that we tolerate, and indeed embrace, a messy multiplicity of museums and museum missions is evidence of the myriad and deep satisfactions of looking at things for ourselves. We needn't always know *why* the prospect of beholding things for ourselves is tantalizing, we just know that it is.

Which makes it even more interesting to ask what is going on from a cognitive perspective. As in the earlier example of looking at a friend's seashell, when we look at things in museums we integrate a vast amount of information, even if we can't fully articulate the knowledge we've gained. In fact, to call it knowledge is misleading: one striking characteristic of the idea of the museum is that it doesn't link the value of the museum experience directly to the amount of knowledge visitors acquire. In other words, while we often expect to learn something in museums, we don't judge the quality of our experience solely by the amount of information we've gained. In fact, the overall cognitive outcome of a museum experience is more often an increased sense of curiosity—of possibility—rather than a sense of fully realized knowledge. Museums large and small have long understood this. Writing in 1849 about the Museum of the Asiatic Society in Calcutta, an unknown librarian captures it perfectly:

The Compiler [the author] is anxious that its scope and purpose should be distinctly understood; that nothing more should be expected from it than just what it assumes to be—a compendious register of the collection of curiosities, comprising names, dates, and just so much of explanation as might awaken, without presuming to gratify, curiosity.[4]

Wunderkammer

The Museum of the Asiatic Society that the Compiler describes—what he calls a "compendious register of the collection of curiosities"—is built on the model of *wunderkammer*, a practice that developed in Renaissance Europe toward the end of the sixteenth century and has shaped the modern idea of the museum ever since.

Wunderkammer means cabinet of curiosities, or cabinet of wonders, or "wonder-room." Created mainly by merchants and aristocrats, they displayed encyclopedic collections of all manner of specimens and exotic objects, carefully grouped and arranged to invite direct observation. Designed to leverage the enticement of looking for oneself, the wunderkammer had many aims: to demonstrate to viewers the erudition of the collector, to display wealth and power, to persuade viewers of the rightness of the collector's typologies and classifications, to stimulate scientific discussion, and to please and dazzle the eye.

One of the earliest well-known illustrations of a cabinet of curiosity is that of Ferrante Imperato, a wealthy apothecary in Naples. In the 1599 print shown in Figure 5.1 you can see Imperato's son pointing out the room's wonders to a pair of visitors while Imperato himself looks on. If you like, take a slow look at the illustration. Give yourself a few minutes to let your eyes wander and linger. What are several things you notice?

There is a lot to see! Here is how one author describes it:

> Every surface of the vaulted ceiling is occupied with preserved fishes, stuffed mammals and curious shells, with a stuffed crocodile suspended in the centre. Examples of corals stand on the bookcases. At the left, the room is fitted out like a studiolo with a range of built-in cabinets whose fronts can be unlocked and let down to reveal intricately fitted nests of pigeonholes forming architectural units, filled with small mineral specimens. Above them, stuffed birds stand against panels inlaid with square polished stone samples, doubtless

Figure 5.1 Cabinet of Curiosities. Engraving from Ferrante Imperato's *Dell'Historia Naturale* (Naples 1599).

Public domain.

marbles and jaspers or fitted with pigeonhole compartments for specimens. Below them, a range of cupboards contain specimen boxes and covered jars.[5]

Wunderkammer dazzled people by not only the sheer range and scope of their collections and the brilliance of their display, but also by the inclusion of rare or freakish biological specimens that challenged classification—a gargantuan cabbage or a bizarrely patterned seashell—and "wonders of nature"—assumed unicorn horns (later determined to be narwhal tusks) or the bones of giants. These objects were so prized that collectors went to great lengths to acquire and attempt to explain them, often relying on elaborate interpretations and fabrication. Chunks of coral were explained as the remains of Gorgons who had been turned into stone; parts of different animals were artfully stitched together and presented as mythological creatures like centaurs, hydra heads, and basilisks.

From a contemporary vantage point, it is easy to dismiss some of these specimens as simple fraud. But to do so may be to miss the complexity of the "wonders" these fabricated pieces intended to reveal, and thus fail to appreciate the subtle ways in which they satisfied the impulse to look for oneself. Renaissance scholar Paula Findlen explains that the more exotic specimens often found in wunderkammer can be considered a kind of *lusus*—Latin for a playful joke or sport or deceit. *Lusus* had two meanings in sixteenth- and seventeenth-century natural history. *Lusus naturae* is a joke of nature—something that nature playfully does when creating the appearance of things, such as shaping a rock to look like a human bone (done by nature as a playful trickery) or fashioning marvelously shaped seashells and brilliantly colored flowers (done by nature as a pleasant amusement). Here, for example, is seventheenth-century collector Lodovico Moscardo describing an unusual stone in his museum that appears to have been painted: "In this stone . . . one sees nature joke with art, since in it she reveals many lines that form the shape of trees, houses, and countrysides, as if the learned hand of a famous painter had sketched them."[6a] Findlen explains that the Renaissance naturalists and collectors "perceived *lusus* to be nature's recreation; by diversifying herself in unusual and surprising ways she [nature] escaped from the weariness of her more mundane tasks, turning the process of creation into an aesthetic experience whose *lusus* was played out in the challenge its artifice gave to art itself."[6b]

A second kind of *lusus* is *lusus scientiae*, which is a joke of knowledge—something the scientist or collector fabricates in order to create an illusion, for example by stitching a taxidermied lamb onto a cornstalk to make a Scythian lamb. For the viewer, pondering whether and how an illusion was created may be part of the viewing experience. An English soldier traveling in Italy in 1664 described such a specimen he saw on display in a Duke's palace:

> A *Hydra* with seven heads, the middle most of which was biggest, and had two canine teeth, and six little ones between, two feet, with four claws on each, and five rows of tubercles on his back. . . . Very probably this *Hydra* was fictitious, the head being like that of a fichet, or of that kind, the body and feet were of a rabbet or hare, and the tail was made of common snakeskin, the back and neck covered with the same.[7]

As Findlen explains, this kind of spectacle "invited the viewer either to participate in the joke, by understanding the subtle transition from

Figure 5.2 Antique depiction of a hydra.
Public domain.

natural to artificial, or to be deceived by it and, in a sense, to become the joke himself."[8] Moreover, in fabricating a "joke of nature"—say by stitching a rooster's beak onto a lizard's body to show a creature that challenges scientific classification—the naturalist-collector might playfully think of himself as imitating how nature worked when she playfully created category-defying *lusus naturae*.

From Erudition to Ogling: P. T. Barnum

The word "museum" has a lofty sound to it—something culturally sanctioned, intellectually worthy. But, as the wunderkammer show, there is a thin line between scholarly appreciation and freakish delight. Alongside museums, plenty of our cultural pastimes leverage the power of people's impulse to look for themselves by intentionally blurring the line between spectacle and scholarship. No one understood this better than the American collector and promoter P.T. Barnum.

Born in 1811, Phineas Taylor Barnum is known mainly for an enterprise he started somewhat later in life, the Barnum & Bailey Circus.

But before starting the circus at the age of 61, Barnum had a long and colorful career as founder and operator of the hugely successful American Museum on lower Broadway in New York City. A disastrous fire took the museum in 1865). Barnum's brilliance was to understand how to combine entertainment, education, and the pleasures of "high" and "low" looking into a single offering. He bought up dusty old wunderkammer collections, combined them with freak show offerings, and served them up to the public in an extravagantly opulent setting that communicated to visitors that they were getting a high-class, erudite experience while at the same time catered to their taste for spectacle.

In a visit to the museum (admission price 25 cents), one could see: extensive shell and rock collections; a vast collection of taxidermied animals from around the world; paintings of American Indians by the artist George Caitlin, along with native American artifacts; the magnificent miniature outfit that General Tom Thumb wore to meet Queen Victoria, and sometimes Tom Thumb himself; live boa constrictors devouring live rabbits; a huge aquarium that held all manner of fishes and two whales. Visitors could have the surface of their head inspected for character traits by "Professor" Livingston, the museum's resident phrenologist; meet the Siamese twins Chang and Eng; and see for themselves the famed FeeJee Mermaid, the mummified remains of a supposedly real female creature but actually the desiccated head of a monkey sewn on to the torso of an orangutan and attached to the back of a fish.

Barnum's museum may have intentionally blurred the line between the scholarly and the spectacular, but the idea of arranging and displaying a dazzlingly vast array of remarkable objects underlies many famous Western encyclopedic museums. The British Museum, the Smithsonian Museum, the Louvre, the Metropolitan Museum: these museums and many, many like them are part of the modern lineage of wunderkammer, reflecting the practice of collecting rare or significant objects that are deemed historically, culturally, aesthetically or scientifically important, and systematically organizing and displaying them for viewers to behold.

Of course, not all museums reflect a wunderkammer sensibility. In fact, the last 40 or so years has seen a big rise in themed museums, which in a sense are the opposite of wunderkammer. Museums like the Canadian Museum of Human Rights in Winnipeg, Canada; the Museum of the Portuguese Language in Sao Paolo, Brazil; the EMP (Experience Music Project) Museum in Seattle, Washington. These museums and museums like them tend to center around immersive experiences rather than physical objects. And because the museums are thematic, their offerings tend not to be as intentionally wide-ranging as wunderkammer. Nonetheless,

Figure 5.3 Barnum's Feejee Mermaid. From *The Life of P. T. Barnum*, Written by Himself, 1855.

Public domain.

themed museums still curate a set of offerings that visitors are invited to experience for themselves.

Do Museums Really Encourage Looking For Oneself?

Even if you accept that the *idea* of the museum is rooted in the attraction of looking or otherwise experiencing things for oneself, if you spend much time in museums you might notice that many museum practices seem to stand in your way of doing so. Wall text tells you what to think and what to look at; audio guides and museum tours draw your attention to certain objects rather than others; exhibits seem designed to make an argument rather than invite speculation; the interior architecture of museum galleries—often with minimal or no seating—seem designed to keep you moving rather than encouraging you to linger. Indeed, to a certain extent these practices are quite common in what we think of as traditional museums—large temple-like urban structures, usually in major cities, that can accommodate masses of people and have vast collections ranging across multiple eras, geographies, and styles. But the fact that museums continue to attract large audiences despite these sometimes-impediments speaks to the magnetism of the idea of museums, however imperfectly realized. The enticing possibility of looking for oneself—especially at things we deem rare or valuable or important—is so alluring that museums needn't perfectly succeed in making it happen in order for this idea to still hold. In fact, in this age of social media, the practice of seeing for oneself has social cachet, as evidenced by the wildly popular practice of taking "selfies" in front of famed museum objects.

The magnetism of the idea of the museum notwithstanding, one could argue that even if museums do a wonderful job of catering to the human impulse to look at things for oneself, they aren't necessarily in the business of helping people develop a capacity for slow looking. There is research that bears this out: studies suggest that visitors spend an average of 15 to 30 seconds in front of a work of art, with a good portion of that time usually spent reading the wall labels.[9]

Our tendency toward fast looking can't entirely be blamed on museums: it is in the nature of human cognition to extract maximum meaning from minimum cognitive effort, as illustrated by the story of the seashell that opened this chapter. A quick glance packs a huge amount of information. But the premise of this book is that purposefully prolonging that first glance and sustaining it over time—even a relatively short time—can bring tremendous rewards, so it is worth looking at museum practices that actually do encourage visitors to move from a cursory glance to sustained observation.

One place to look for such practices is in the offerings of a museum's education department. Ironically, because it is generally but mistakenly assumed that young people need more support to engage in sustained observation than adults do, these practices are most likely to be found in museum offerings for young people.

Visual Inquiry Programs in Museums

In the East wing of the National Gallery of Art in Washington D.C., a group of fifth graders from a local public school sits in a semicircle in front of the Shaw Memorial, a massive bronze-patina relief sculpture that commemorates Colonel Robert Gould Shaw and the men of the 54th Massachusetts, the first Civil War enlisted regiment of African Americans. A museum guide stands slightly to the side of the sculpture and leads the group in an exploration of the work. "Let your eyes scan the whole surface of the sculpture," she says. "What are the main things that catch your eye, and what are some of the details that take a little bit longer to notice?" The students are quiet for a moment, and then begin pointing out several obvious features of the work, such as the horses, and the men riding them. The guide encourages them to continue, asking, "What else do you see?"

A student raises her hand and says, "I see diagonal lines." The guide asks where she sees them. "On the people's legs," the student responds, "and on the horses' legs." Suddenly several more hands shoot up, and the students start wriggling with eagerness to be called on. One student points out the diagonal lines of the guns and sweeps her hand up and down at an angle, indicating their directionality. Another student points out the diagonal lines of the drumsticks beating on the drum. Soon the students begin pointing out more details in the work—"the lady up top" and the stars above her, the "sleeping bag or something rolled up on people's backs." The guide keeps encouraging the students to look closely, but at this point they need little prompting. Making new observations has become exciting for them, and each new detail they notice spurs them on to notice yet another and another. Eventually, when the students' epicycles of observation wind down, the guide turns the conversation toward interpreting the work. "What do you think is going on in the sculpture?" she asks, and as students formulate their answers she urges them to connect their observations to the explanations they offer.

This real-life story comes from Art Around the Corner, a program at the National Gallery of Art that works with Washington D.C.-area elementary schools, particularly schools that serve students from low-income families.[10] The program takes what is often called a visual inquiry-based approach to learning in museums—an approach that has been on the rise in museums for a couple of decades. The basic idea is to structure an experience in which visitors are invited to make their own observations of works of art and other museum objects, and then to let those observations stimulate their curiosity and drive the development of their own questions and interpretations. The approach has gained popularity as an alternative to traditional, didactic approaches to museum learning in which groups of children and adults might be shepherded around the museum by a knowledgeable guide who imparts facts and pointedly tells viewers what to look at. In contrast, an inquiry-based experience begins by asking viewers what *they* notice and what questions *they* have.

Visual inquiry-based programs in museums are a special application of a broader educational approach popular in schools that goes by various names, including problem-based learning, interest-driven learning, and (sometimes) student-centered learning. Originally developed in the context of science education, its goal is to make learning more meaningful and intrinsically interesting to learners by encouraging them to ask questions they are genuinely interested in, and then using those questions as a basis for inquiry. Underlying inquiry-based learning is the educational philosophy of *constructivism*, which is the view that people learn best by constructing their own understanding of the world through an iterative process of interest-driven experience and reflection.

It can be tempting to reduce inquiry-based learning to the simple idea that students rather than teachers should choose the topics they want to explore. This is true as far as it goes, but it fails to acknowledge the dispositional side of the story. As a teacher writing on the educational website Edutopia, puts it, "Inquiry-based learning is more than asking a student what he or she wants to know. It's about triggering curiosity."[11] This comment underscores an important connection between inquiry-based learning and looking for oneself, which is that the impulse to look for oneself is both a sign and a stimulant of curiosity. It is a sign of curiosity in the most basic sense, because experiencing the sensation of the impulse is what signals to us that we are interested in something. It is a stimulant for curiosity because looking for oneself is a form of direct engagement. It visually connects us to objects in the world and positions us to care about seeing or learning more about them. We see this latter point in action in the story of the students and the Shaw Memorial. One student points out the diagonal lines of the guns; other students turn their attention to look for themselves, which sparks their curiosity to look for more diagonal lines in the work, which in turn draws them into noticing other details.

The term "inquiry" means a "looking into" something, which is precisely what prolonged observation is. Sometimes the term is used to describe a process with a specific end point or goal, such as a scientific inquiry into the causes of a particular phenomenon, or a police inquiry into the facts behind a crime. But inquiry can also be open-ended—a looking-into that creates its own path as it unfolds—which is what happens with the students and the Shaw Memorial. This process of being drawn down a path of unfolding observations points to another important connection between looking for oneself and inquiry-based learning: as looking for oneself unfolds into prolonged observation, it *is* a form of inquiry. Pushing the eye to look more closely, to look for detail, to make new discoveries and nuanced discernments, is itself a mode of inquiry because it moves the act of observation along a path of discovery.

Many museums use an inquiry-based approach in their educational programming. Some do so informally while others use a structured educational program. One such program, used in probably hundreds of art museums in the United States and around the world, is called Visual Thinking Strategies, known more commonly by its acronym VTS.[12]

In VTS, a facilitator leads a group conversation about a work of art by using three specific yet open-ended questions: "What's going on in this picture? What do you see that makes you say that? What more can we find?" Looking for oneself is interwoven with VTS. Before the first question is even asked, students are encouraged to look closely at a work of art and describe what they see, and throughout the process they are encouraged to continue to look carefully at the artwork, to describe their observations in detail, and to back up their ideas with visual evidence they perceive in the work. The strategy is simple, powerful, and effective: students readily engage in the structured discussion; they are genuinely encouraged to look for themselves, and in a true inquiry-based spirit they inquire about the meaning of the artwork by pursuing observations, questions, and ideas that they themselves raise.

One reason the VTS strategy works so well is that students easily understand the three core questions. The language is familiar to them and they easily understand what the questions are asking, in large part because the questions follow a pattern of thinking that is familiar to any school-aged child: reasoning with evidence. The question "What is going on in this picture?" asks students to form an interpretation. The question "What do you see that makes you say that?" asks students to provide direct visual evidence to support their interpretation. Students may not necessarily be familiar with the technical language of reasoning—words like evidence and interpretation—but even young children understand the basic pattern of thinking involved in trying to answer these questions.

Encouraging viewers to look for themselves and to follow natural patterns of thinking is a mainstay of inquiry-based approaches in museums, and another such approach is called Artful Thinking.[13] This is the approach used in the foregoing example from the National Gallery of Art. Like VTS, Artful Thinking uses short, easy-to-understand strategies to guide viewers' explorations of works of art. But instead of centering on a single core reasoning strategy, as VTS does, it includes several strategies or "thinking routines" that invite viewers to explore works of art in various ways. For example, the thinking routine used by the National Gallery museum guide is called "See-Think-Wonder." It is a three-step process that guides students through a sequence of first making many observations about an artwork (See), then developing interpretations (Think), and finally brainstorming several questions about the work (Wonder). Other thinking routines in the Artful Thinking program focus in on specific aspects of active looking. For example, the thinking routine enacted by the "Looking 10 × 2—try this" activity in Chapter 2, emphasizes close observation and provides a structure for looking closely at an artwork for a prolonged period of time, then doubling back and looking at it anew. A routine called "Creative Questions" helps viewers expand their understanding of the complexity of an artwork by guiding them to ask several different kinds of questions about it.[14]

In general, I am a big fan of inquiry-based approaches in museums. In my professional life, I have participated in the development of Artful Thinking and conducted research on the effects of both Artful Thinking and VTS.[15] I like these and similar inquiry-based approaches because they work: when used well, they dramatically increase people's engagement with works of art. Countless times in classrooms, museums, and workshop settings I have watched groups of people use inquiry-based approaches to engage in a 20- or 30-minute passionate discussion about a work of art that in another circumstance they might have walked right by. In essence, the programs work because they strategically build on people's impulse to look at things for themselves by providing useful structures to prolong observation. But while these programs are powerful, they also raise genuine challenges. First and foremost is the challenge of information.

Information is Tricky

A basic tenet of inquiry-based approaches is that they begin with viewers' own observations and often encourage them to engage with artworks for an extended period without necessarily receiving facts about the works that some might regard as essential. So, for example, in the earlier example of the Shaw Memorial, the fifth graders spend quite a bit of time looking closely, sharing observations, and discussing what they think about the work, before key information about the memorial is offered—such as its title and what it depicts. This isn't to say that the information would be withheld from the students if asked. But they don't happen to ask, engaged as they are in the activity of looking. Instead, students tend to become captivated by the visual information offered directly by the work itself, and by developing questions and ideas based on their own discernments and insights. But critics of the approach worry that viewers may develop interpretations that are misguided and ill informed, thus cheating them out of an authentic experience.[16]

The role of information in inquiry-based approaches is an oft-debated issue amongst museum professionals. Several years ago there was a memorable public discussion about it between two well-known museum educators that was subsequently published in the journal *Curator*.[17] The educators were Danielle Rice, then senior curator of education of the Philadelphia Art Museum, and Philip Yenawine, former director of education at the Museum of Modern Art and a co-developer of the VTS program.

Representing the VTS approach, Philip Yenawine takes somewhat of a purist stance when he talks about the role of information in visual inquiry. He prefers not to transmit any information to young viewers before they engage with a work. Instead, he puts the onus on educators to select appropriate works that can be experienced without external information and to carefully facilitate the discussion so that viewers look closely and make the most out of the visual information directly available to them. Like Yenawine, Danielle Rice wants to encourage close looking. But she believes that her job is to share her own knowledge and expertise in order to enhance viewers' experience, and she aims to layer information into a discussion so that viewers can truly advance their understanding of a work. Rice acknowledges that, "we have to be very thoughtful about what kinds of information we bring to bear when helping novice viewers make sense of art. Too often we flood our viewers with the wrong kind of data and basically turn their analytical process off." She goes on to explain:

> I have found that the best use of information is to reinforce and underline viewers' natural responses to a work of art. For example, if viewers suspect that a painting of a mother and child may have had some kind of religious significance, I can tell them that indeed the work represents the Virgin Mary holding the Infant Jesus. In this way I use the information to validate the viewers' response and encourage them to analyze further.[18]

Philip Yenawine pushes back a bit. "It depends on what you mean by 'information'," he responds:

> Viewers dig deeply into the information contained in the image, which is very important to me. Understanding art, not to mention having aesthetic experience, starts with engaging deeply in what is presented to us by artists. What the process I teach omits is what I call the "information surround": facts and opinions about the picture that are not apparent in the image, such as information about the artist's life. Or how the object was made. . . . Or meanings ascribed by those who know art history.[19]

Yenawine goes on to explain that for beginning viewers he recommends "selecting images from which viewers' own observations are likely to be what the artist had in mind for us to observe." He points out that:

> Even with this intention, there is a lot of choice—from some Egyptian figures to many Japanese prints to some tapestries, or paintings by Bruegel, Goya, Cassatt, or Kahlo and legions of photographers, to suggest just a few. Beginning viewers can discuss such images without any intervention from me and interpret them richly without need for additional information.[20]

In essence, this is a disagreement about pedagogical technique rather than viewer experience. Both Rice and Yenawine want viewers to have an authentic and engaging experience with a work of art. They also both want viewers to experience the impulse to look for themselves and to find reward in doing so—the reward being both the advancement of understanding and the excitement of discovery. But their opinions differ as to the effect of information on viewers' achievement of that reward. My own view is that neither extreme is tenable over the long term: a constant feed of information will eventually stultify the impulse to look for oneself, but looking for oneself over time often leads to a desire for more information and it would be counterproductive to withhold it.

As I suggested above, I have seen enough visual inquiry-based discussions in action to know how engaged viewers become when they have a chance to really look deeply for themselves—and to witness how nuanced their observations become as they unfold in a context temporarily unconstrained by external information. It should be no surprise that I tend toward the "less is more" side of the spectrum, since this book's premise is that a tremendous amount of learning occurs when we simply take the time to look beyond a quick glance. But the question about the role of information can't be ignored. If a case is to be made for slow looking, not only as an important mode of learning, but also one that can be *taught*, then educators need practical approaches for how to fold external information into students' experience of direct observation in ways that enhance rather than subvert the gains from slow looking. Visual inquiry-based models are one such approach, whether practiced in a highly structured way, as in VTS, or in a more organic, iterative way as described by Danielle Rice.

It is noteworthy that the museum experiences Yenawine and Rice have in mind during their conversation are mainly *facilitated* experiences. Led by an educator who has a plan and a structure to carry them out, they usually involve groups of learners and group discussions. Structurally they are more akin to what happens in school than to what happens in a less structured stroll through a museum gallery. Which brings us to the topic of the next chapter. This chapter has argued that museums are widespread cultural institutions of learning that have thrived in the modern age because they offer a huge variety of ways to sample the cognitive pleasures of seeing things for oneself—and that there is a magnetism to the idea of the museum that serves to hold together a surprisingly diverse collection of enterprises. The next chapter turns to another cultural institution of learning, even more widespread than museums, that has an equally magnetic hold on the public imagination: the institution of school.

Notes

1   *Museums of the World.* (2012). Berlin, Boston: De Gruyter Saur. Retrieved 3 Dec. 2016, from http://www.degruyter.com/view/product/180440.
2   Quoted in Alexander, E. P. & Alexander, M. (2008). *Museums in Motion: An Introduction to the History and Functions of Museums.* Lanham, MD: AltaMira Press.
3   Weil, S. (1999). From being about something to being for somebody: The ongoing transformation of the American museum. *Daedalus 128*(3), 229–258.
4   Unknown author. (1849). *Catalogue of Curiosities in the Museum of the Asiatic Society, Calcutta.* Calcutta, India: J. Thomas, Baptist Mission Press.
5   Retrieved from https://en.wikipedia.org/wiki/Cabinet_of_curiosities.
6a Quoted in Findlen, P. (1990). Jokes of nature and jokes of knowledge: The playfulness of scientific discourse in Early Modern Europe. *Renaissance Quarterly 43*(2), 292–331.
6b Ibid, p. 298.
7   Ibid, p. 319.

8   Ibid, p. 319.
9   A 2001 study of visitors to the Metropolitan Museum of Art found that the mean time spent viewing a work of art was 27.2 seconds, with a median time of 17.0 seconds. See Smith, J. K. & Smith, L. F. (2001). Spending time on art. *Empirical Studies of the Arts 19*(2), 229–236.
10 For more information about Art Around the Corner, see http://www.nga.gov/content/ngaweb/education/teachers/art-around-the-corner.html. The story described is captured in a video produced by the National Gallery of Art that can be found on their website.
11 Wolpert-Gawron, H. (2016, Aug. 11). "What the heck is inquiry-based learning?" *Edutopia*. Retrieved from http://www.edutopia.org/blog/what-heck-inquiry-based-learning-heather-wolpert-gawron.
12 See http://www.vtshome.org/.
13 For more information about Artful Thinking, see http://pzartfulthinking.org/.
14 See http://pzartfulthinking.org/.
15 See Tishman, S. & Palmer, P. (2007). Works of art are good to think about: A study of the impact of the Artful Thinking program on students' and teachers' concepts of art, and students' concepts of thinking. In *Evaluating the Impact of Arts and Cultural Education* (89–101). Paris: Centre Pompidou.
16 See, for example, Burnham, R. & Kai-Kee, E. (2011). *Teaching in the Art Museum: Interpretation as Experience*. Los Angeles: J. Paul Getty Museum.
17 Rice, D. & Yenawine, P. (2002). A conversation on object-centered learning in art museums. *Curator: The Museum Journal 45*(4), 289–301.
18 Ibid, p. 296.
19 Ibid, p. 293.
20 Ibid, p. 293.

CHAPTER 6

Looking Goes to School

Museums and schools have this in common—like the idea of the museum, the idea of school admits of huge variety. Just as there are all kinds of museums that foreground a wide array of collections and experiences, there are all kinds of schools that vary widely in what, how, and who they teach. As with museums, there is a central organizing principle that unifies the idea of school. But unlike museums, it isn't the idea that there is irreplaceable value in looking at things for oneself. Instead, it is the idea that there is value in following an organized pattern of instruction in order to learn effectively. This pattern of instruction might be called a curriculum, a syllabus, a plan of study, or it may not have a formal name at all. It might be designed in advance and applied to many students equally—such as a core curriculum—or it might be emergent and coalesce into a pattern bit by bit in response to an individual student's developing experience, such as in a mentorship or coaching program. But no matter how instruction is developed or applied, the idea that learning can be produced, accelerated, or improved by following an organized pattern of instruction is at the heart of the idea of school.

It is notable that the core idea behind museums—the idea that there is unique cognitive value in looking at things for oneself—isn't necessarily part of the idea of school. In fact, the stock image commonly associated with school is a teacher standing at the front of a classroom lecturing to rows of front-facing students which is in stark contrast to the idea of looking for oneself. But a belief in the cognitive benefit of looking for oneself does play a central role in several historical philosophies of schooling, and it is interesting to trace its thread.

The First Picture Book

By the mid-seventeenth century, the Czech pastor John Amos Comenius was already a famous figure in Europe. He was known as a spirited theologian, a distinguished philosopher, and, in what would be his most lasting legacy, a visionary teacher and education reformer. Originally from Moravia, Comenius's Protestant-leaning religious views kept him on the run from counter-reformation forces in Europe, and he and his family moved around quite a bit, living for a time in England, Sweden, Transylvania, Hungary, and the Netherlands. But despite frequent upheaval, Comenius always found time to write and teach, and his views about the importance of universal education, along with his views about what might today be called a child-centered pedagogy, kept him in demand by officials who were eager to establish enlightened programs of education in England, Sweden, and Poland. In 1657, at the height of his prodigious career, Comenius published *Orbis Sensualium Pictus*; in English, *The World of Things Obvious to the Senses Drawn in Pictures*. The book, which was written in high Dutch and immediately translated into English, is often considered to be the first instructional picture book for children. Over the next two centuries it would become one of the most widely used textbooks in the world.

The central idea behind the *Orbis Pictus* is that children learn naturally by experiencing the world directly through their senses, and that formal education should capitalize on this fact. The book is filled with pictures of things that would have formed part of children's everyday experience, including singing birds and grazing sheep, and common trade and household activities like bread-baking, fishing, and blacksmithing.

Orbis Pictus bills itself as a picture book, but as its full title indicates, it is about learning from all the senses, and it starts right in with a multisensory approach to teaching children the alphabet. According to the instructions that Comenius gives in the Preface, children will learn their letters first by looking at a picture of an animal. Then, they will hear the person reading the book aloud make the sound of the animal, which corresponds to the letter pictured alongside the animal (e.g., The Duck Quaketh). This combination of visual and auditory stimulus, Comenius believes, serves to anchor the idea of the letter in the child's mind. As instruction proceeds, children will be encouraged to copy the pictures by hand, so as to continue to learn directly from the senses through the act of drawing.

Comenius's big insight was that looking and otherwise sensing for oneself is both sensorily pleasing and cognitively powerful. It would be

(3)

Cornix cornicatur, *á á*   A a
The Crow crieth.

Agnus balat,   *b é é é*   B b
The Lamb blaiteth.

Cicáda ſtridet,   *cí cí*   C c
The Graſhopper chirpeth.

Upupa dicit,   *du du*   D d
The Whooppoo ſaith.

Infans ejulat,   *é é é*   E e
The Infant crieth.

Ventus flat,   *fi fi*   F f
The Wind bloweth.

Anſer gingrit,   *ga ga*   G g
The Gooſe gagleth.

Os halat,   *há'h há'h*   H h
The mouth breatheth out.

Mus mintrit,   *í í í*   I i
The Mouſe chirpeth.

Anas tetrinnit, *kha kha*   K k
The Duck quaketh.

Lupus ululat,   *lu ulu*   L l
The Wolf howleth.

Urſus murmurat, *mum mum*   M m
The Bear grumbleth.

B 2   Felis

Figure 6.1 Page from Johann Amos Comenius's *Orbis Sensualium Pictus*, 1705.
Public domain.

an overreach to claim that Comenius is explicitly making an argument similar to the argument made in the previous chapter—that the cognitive power of looking for oneself partly has to do with the huge amount of integrated information that is hard to acquire efficiently in other ways. But it seems possible that Comenius would be sympathetic to this view. Here is the rationale Comenius himself offers in the book's Preface for why children should learn through the senses, and in particular by looking at pictures:

> I. To entice witty children to it, that they may not conceit a torment to be in the school, but dainty fare. For it is apparent, that children (even from their infancy almost) are delighted with Pictures, and willingly please their eyes with these lights:

> II. This same little Book will serve to stir up the Attention, which is to be fastened upon things, and even to be sharpened more and more: which is also a great matter. For the Senses (being the main guides of childhood, because therein the mind doth not as yet raise up itself to an abstracted contemplation of things) evermore seek their own objects, and if they be away, they grow dull, and wry themselves hither and thither out of a weariness of themselves: but when their objects are present, they grow merry, wax lively, and willingly suffer themselves to be fastened upon them, till the thing be sufficiently discerned. This Book then will do a good piece of service in taking (especially flickering) wits, and preparing them for deeper studies.[1]

Does Comenius think that the process of looking at pictures yields valuable direct knowledge, or does he see the cognitive power of looking for oneself as merely a stepping stone to more abstract thinking? It's hard to say. On the one hand, he tells us that the senses can be "fastened upon [objects], till the thing be sufficiently discerned." On the other, he argues that the child's mind "doth not as yet raise up itself to an abstracted contemplation of things," and that looking at pictures will thus "prepare them for deeper studies."

What does seem clear is that Comenius believed that looking directly at pictures is intrinsically engaging, and that children "willingly please their eyes with these lights." It also seems clear that Comenius viewed learning through direct visual perception as fundamental to children's nature: "For it is apparent, that children (even from their infancy almost) are delighted with Pictures." And he further believed that instruction should be organized to take advantage of this fact, as evidenced by his authorship of *Orbis Pictus*.

"Education According to Nature"

A century later, the idea that education should be designed to build on children's natural sensory tendencies was taken up and expanded by the philosopher Jean-Jacques Rousseau, who famously made the case for "education according to nature."

Like Comenius, Rousseau recognized the strength of human impulse to learn from sensory experience. And because he believed that people are born good but ultimately corrupted by society, he believed that the naturalness of our impulse to learn from the senses gives it a moral as well as epistemological authority. In a Rousseauian world, a child learns about the nature of reality, and at the same time learns to be a good person, through an early education that affords extensive direct contact with the physical world (preferably in natural settings rather than the city), and is based primarily on learning from the senses.

Looking for oneself is obviously a form of direct contact with the physical world, since the eyes are a sense organ, and Rousseau clearly supports direct observation as a form of sensory learning. That said, his main emphasis is on physically interactive forms of sensory learning in which the body experiments with objects in the world and learns through the sensorily experienced consequences. In his book *Emile*, Rousseau lays out his view of an ideal education in a fictional story about a boy named Emile. In a famous passage he explains:

> Your ill-tempered child ruins everything he touches. Do not get angry; put what he can damage out of his reach. He breaks the furniture he uses. Do not hurry to replace it for him. Let him feel the disadvantage of being deprived of it. He breaks the windows of his room; let the wind blow on him night and day without worrying about colds. . . . Never complain about the inconveniences he causes you, but make him be the one to feel those inconveniences first.[2]

For Rousseau, the child's trial-and-error sensory impulses are natural, and in an "education according to nature," following such impulses naturally leads to learning, especially when rightly guided by an adult. But there are also other natural ways children learn—ways that don't necessarily foreground the sensory experimentation Rousseau emphasizes—such as watching and imitating the everyday behavior of adults or engaging in imaginative play. The impulse to look for oneself is clearly a natural sensory impulse—perhaps even more than the impulse to break furniture. But its significance to learning is not only that it comes naturally, but also—and perhaps more importantly—that it tends to produce a high cognitive yield. In other words, by looking at things for ourselves we acquire and integrate multiple kinds of information in a rapid and vivid way.

Rousseau's ideas about the power of sensory learning are inclusive of looking for oneself, and in a sense require it. It is even possible to argue that breaking the furniture *is* a kind of looking for oneself, to the extent that it is a direct exploration of the sensible qualities of things—which is how Rousseau seems to want to construe it. But unlike Comenius, Rousseau doesn't go to great lengths to emphasize observation. His philosophy accommodates it, but he doesn't distinguish learning through looking from learning through more physically interactive sensory experiences that involve concrete trial and error. Nor does he emphasize the simple delight children take in the act of looking. Nonetheless, Rousseau's emphasis on "education according to nature" and learning through the senses shaped the views of educators for centuries to come, including educators who had a lively interest in the role of observation in learning.

Children at the Center

One such educator was Johann Heinrich Pestalozzi. Strongly influenced by Rousseau's philosophy and by his own deep sympathy for orphans and children in poverty, Pestalozzi spent a lifetime developing an educational philosophy that aimed to educate children's "hearts, hands and minds." His most famous school, which he founded in Yverdon, Switzerland in 1802, attracted international attention and was reputedly visited by thousands of Europeans and Americans who wished to observe its distinctive pedagogy.

If you walked into the school at Yverdon, you might see children of different ages clustered in small groups engaged in a range of activities. One group might be examining an object, while another works at a craft. Some children might be listening to an informal lecture by a teacher, while still more are outdoors in the schoolyard working in a garden or exploring nature. What you probably wouldn't see is children lined up in rows quietly attending to a schoolmaster, hands folded in their laps, passively absorbing information. The warm, active, child-centered approach

Figure 6.2 Conrad Ermisch: "Pestalozzi in His School at Neuhof", 1882.

at Yverdon placed the child's direct sensory experience at the center of the learning experience, and became known as the Pestalozzi method. Its fundamental precept was to mold the curriculum to the child's natural interests and unfolding development, rather than the more traditional other way around.

One element of the Pestalozzi method was *object lessons*. These were prolonged activities in which children looked closely at objects from their own familiar surroundings—the land outside the schoolroom, a rock, a peppercorn, a leaf, a flower. The children would be encouraged to take ample time to observe, describe, and sketch the objects, in order to fully perceive their sensory qualities. In doing so, they raised questions and made discoveries that would lead them, through induction, to increasingly abstract ideas about the properties of the objects—ideas knitted together by the threads of the children's own perceptions.

The object lesson (sometimes called *object theory*) is based on Pestalozzi's belief that people learn best what is most immediately present to them— particularly what is present through the senses—and that strengthening students' perceptive faculties laid the foundation for the development of abstract knowledge. This in itself may sound a little dry. But, as visitors' descriptions of the school at Yverdon attest, Pestalozzian education is infused with a warmth for children, and a genuine appreciation of their capacity to look for themselves. The Pestalozzi method is not so much a prescriptive series of steps as it is a general reorientation away from a dry and didactic approach to teaching in which the teacher's job is to impart information, and toward a student-centered approach in which teachers build on children's firsthand experiences to guide them gently into the world of ideas.

There are two important ways that Pestalozzi's views connect to the impulse to look for oneself. The first, of course, is Pestalozzi's emphasis on direct observation, which *is* looking for oneself. The second is Pestalozzi's strong emphasis on the self as the author of knowledge. Pestalozzi believed that it was natural for children to want to make their own observations, and that they could acquire true and deep know-ledge by doing so. Perhaps more than any educator mentioned in this chapter, Pestalozzi comes closest to three of the central arguments of this book, which are: 1) that the impulse to look at things for oneself is natural and intrinsically engaging; 2) that direct observation yields complex understandings, even to the untrained eye; and 3) that from the stand-point of learning there are great gains in prolonging the experience of looking.

Pestalozzi's idea that the child's own experience should be at the center of her education has had a profound influence on education theorists and practitioners in the last two centuries. It gave rise to the progressive movement in education, and is perhaps most fully developed in the philosophy of John Dewey. Later in this chapter we will take a closer look at the connections between Dewey's ideas and the form of direct observation that Pestalozzi emphasized, but first there are a few interesting stories to tell. The first two stories are about how the emphasis on pro-longed observational engagement with objects found expression in the work of two nineteenth-century educators who taught at opposite ends of the age spectrum—Friedrich Froebel, a student of Pestalozzi's who is often called the father of kindergarten, and Louis Agassiz, a scientist, educator, and the founder of the Museum of Comparative Zoology at Harvard University where he became renowned for his innovative teaching style with graduate students.

Froebel and His Gifts

When he was still a young man and new to the teaching profession, Friedrich Froebel went twice to Yverdon to study with Pestalozzi— once briefly in 1805 when he was 24, and again for several months in 1807. The visits had a lasting influence. Froebel was particularly impressed by the practice of object lessons, and by the warm and supportive learning environment of the school. Over the next three decades Froebel continued to develop his views on education, and in 1837 he started a "play and activity" institute for young children in Germany that embodied his central ideas. He called the school a *kindergarten*—a child garden.

Froebel's great insight was that play and creative self-expression are powerful forms of learning. Accordingly, activities in the child's garden included song, storytelling, imaginative play, and lots of playful exploration of physical objects and materials. As part of the curriculum, Froebel introduced a series of "gifts." These were simple physical objects designed to stimulate learningful play that were offered to children in a sequence over time. The first gift was a set of six soft worsted wool balls on a string. The second was a set of three wooden shapes—a sphere, a cube, and a cylinder. The third was a set of eight small wooden cubes; the fourth a set of eight rectangular blocks.

The idea was that when children were playing with the gifts— touching them, rolling them, stacking them—they would discover their distinct physical properties, which in turn would lead them to abstract ideas. For instance, playing with the sphere, cube and cylinder together was supposed encourage the child to develop the concept of opposites and combinations—the sphere and cube being opposites and the cylinder being their synthesis. As Froebel explains:

> My educational method offers to its pupils from the beginning the opportunity to collect their own experiences from the things themselves, to look with their own eyes and learn by their own experiments to know things and the relations of things to each other.[3]

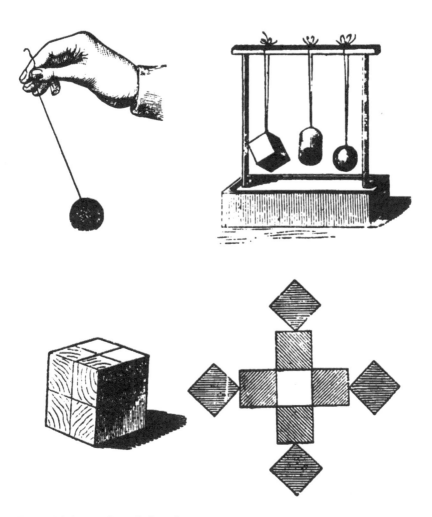

Figure 6.3 Some of Froebel's Gifts.
Public domain.

Like Pestalozzi, Froebel believed children should be the author of their own knowledge through direct observation and self-guided activity. Where he went further than Pestalozzi was to emphasize the elemental power of play.

The fact that playful self-activity is what we expect to see in contemporary kindergartens is a testimony to the power and spread of Froebel's ideas. But in the mid-nineteenth century, the idea that teachers should structure their lessons around self-directed play was so counter to the prevailing concept of school that there was actually an exhibit of a Froebelian classroom at the 1876 World's Fair in Philadelphia that aimed to show visitors what this novel idea looked like in practice. Children from a local orphanage—poignantly named the Northern Home for Friendless Children—were installed in a model kindergarten classroom and encouraged to play with the Froebel gifts, gently guided by two young women teachers. Spectators looked on from behind a railing, often lingering for hours to watch and to question the teachers about their methods when day's lessons ended. It was reputedly one of the most popular exhibits at the fair.

"Study Nature, not Books"

Three years earlier and a few hundred miles to the northeast, there was another short-lived experiment in education that had a similarly outsized impact. In the summer of 1873 on a tiny wind-scoured island in Buzzards Bay in Massachusetts, the renowned scientist Louis Agassiz established the Anderson School of Natural History, so named for John Anderson, a wealthy New York merchant who donated the rocky island to Agassiz's project. The school was intended to serve as a kind of summer field station and its purpose was to help public school teachers learn about natural history—and how to teach it—by studying with Agassiz and experiencing his pedagogical methods. Here is how the school was described in a letter to the editor in the journal *Nature* in 1874:

> Courses of instructive lectures in various branches of natural history should be delivered by the seaside . . . during the summer months . . . by Agassiz himself, and by other naturalists belonging either to the same institution [Harvard University], or to other scientific establishments in the United States, who combined together to assist him. The object of these courses was chiefly for the benefit of teachers proposing to introduce the study of natural history into their schools, and for such students as preparing to become teachers.[4]

Agassiz, already 72 years old at the time, was a public figure who was well known both a as a scientist and educator. Born in Switzerland, his early geological work in the Alps on the movement of glacial ice sheets eventually brought him on a lecture tour to the United States, which was so successful that Harvard offered him a professorship. There, as a zoology professor and avid collector of natural specimens, Agassiz founded the Museum of Comparative Zoology—a museum which bears the stamp of his vision of natural history to this day.[5]

Agassiz's pedagogical methods were legendary. Indeed, from the perspective of slow looking, he might be characterized as an extreme practitioner. When students arrived at Agassiz's lab at Harvard, eager to study with the great man, he would begin by handing them some sort of natural specimen—often a fish skeleton—and instruct them to go off and observe it carefully. They would do so, and when they would report back to him in a few hours with their results, he would tell them to keep on looking. And looking and looking and looking. In an oft-told tale, student Samuel Scudder recalled his frustration, and eventually his illumination, as Agassiz repeatedly made him return to his observation of a fish, day after day. Scudder struggled mightily to find new features to observe:

> I pushed my finger down its throat to feel how sharp the teeth were. I began to count the scales in the different rows, until I was convinced that that was nonsense. At last a happy thought struck me—I would draw the fish; and now with surprise I began to discover new features in the creature.[6]

Scudder's experience was typical. William James, who as a young man travelled with Agassiz on a voyage up the Amazon, offered this recollection at a scientific gathering at the museum, two decades after Agassiz's death:

> There is probably no public school teacher now in New England who will not tell you how Agassiz used to lock a student up in a room full of turtle shells, or lobster shells, or oyster shells, without a book or word to help him, and not let him out till he had discovered all the truth which the objects contained. Others never found them . . . "Go to Nature; take the facts into your own hands; look, and see for yourself!"—these were the maxims which Agassiz preached wherever he went, and their effect on pedagogy was electric.[7]

Despite his many scientific credentials, when Agassiz was introduced, he preferred to be called simply Louis Agassiz, teacher, and his great cause was the teaching of natural history. He railed against science instruction that was based on studying books and memorizing facts, and he passionately encouraged the direct study of nature, which he believed had a threefold benefit: it yielded genuine and meaningful knowledge of the natural world; it accorded with the natural human impulse to see things for oneself; and it elevated the spirit by connecting man to nature. Agassiz wanted students of natural history to make nature their textbook, and he liked to say that "if you study nature in books, when you go out of doors you cannot find her."[8] More than any other scientist of the time, he wanted to popularize the study of natural history, and his goal was to radically reshape the way science was taught—not just in universities but in public education as well. Toward this end—and very unusually—he opened his lectures at Harvard to the public, and especially encouraged public school teachers, including women, to attend.

What was important about the Anderson School of Natural History was that it widened the already wide influence of Agassiz's view about the importance of studying nature directly. In an announcement advertising the school, Agassiz said:

> I do not propose to give much instruction in matters which may be learned from books. I want, on the contrary, to prepare those who shall attend to observe for themselves. I would therefore advise all those who wish only to be taught natural history in the way in which it is generally talk, buy recitations, to give up their intention of joining the school.[9]

Agassiz brought with him to Penikese many students and instructors who already were, or who would become, leading scientists and influential educators. These people helped to spread Agassiz's ideas, and the fame of the school was also likely burnished by the unfortunate fact that it was Agassiz's last great project: he died the following December, and although his son Alexander, also a highly accomplished scientist, ran the school for one more summer season, the project fizzled out. (It should be noted that Alexander Agassiz did very successfully continue his family's connection to the Museum of Comparative Zoology, where he served as a curator, benefactor and director for another 40 years.)

Although by some measures Louis Agassiz's pedagogical methods may seem extreme, they are rooted in a similar idea that underlies this book, namely that a huge amount of learning can occur when the moment of observation is expanded beyond first glance. It is within this expanded space that the many benefits of slow and careful looking have time to accrue, and the accrual is due in large part to the self-authored nature of prolonged observation. As Agassiz would say, "take the facts into your own hands, and look for yourself."

The Nature Study Movement

Agassiz's advice to "study nature, not books," took hold of the public imagination and became the motto of a newly emerging movement in American education—the nature study movement. Although Agassiz didn't live long enough to see his dictum metamorphose into a widespread phenomenon, nor even to hear the term 'nature-study movement,' he was regarded as the movement's hero and inspirational father.

The central idea behind nature study was to get people outdoors into nature so they could connect intellectually and spiritually with their immediate natural environment, mainly through close observation of the plants and animals of daily life. The movement was framed as a combination of scientific investigation and the development of sentiment, and, like many progressive ideas at the end of the nineteenth century, it became popular against the backdrop of the increasing mechanization of modern life. The proponents of nature study viewed a connection to nature as an antidote to the deadening forces of consumerism and industrialization: by studying nature, people—and especially young people—could rekindle humankind's intuitive connection to the natural world, and at the same time develop the intellectual capacities required of science. Nature study was at once modern and ancient. As Kevin Armitage explains in his impressive history of the nature study movement: "Nature study advocates sought to embrace the modern world of science while retaining the older methods of fellowship with nature that yielded the unique experiences and ethical insights that science could not."[10]

For more than three decades spanning the late nineteenth and early twentieth centuries, nature study was astoundingly popular; it gripped the public imagination both as an educational movement and a cultural pastime. Armitage describes:

> Armed with guide books, cameras, collecting jars, and unre-strained curiosity, Americans flocked from their homes and classrooms to nearby forests, prairies, rivers, and mountains to gain greater insight into the wondrous workings of nature. "Nature study", as it enthusiasts dubbed the movement, used instruction in basic natural history, such as plant identification, animal life histories, and school gardens, to promote the skills needed to succeed in industrial life and to cultivate the spiritual growth in modern life occluded.[11]

At its height, nature study was taught in public schools in every state in America. Many states offered statewide nature study curricula, and several states made it a requirement. Part of its lasting legacy is the presence of science as a required subject in elementary school. However, one way that nature study differentiated itself from traditional science teaching was by emphasizing the interconnectedness of the natural world. Its practitioners advocated studying plants and animals in relation to one another as part of a living environment rather than as isolated specimens in a laboratory. In this way, the nature study movement laid the foundation for the 20th century growth of scientific and humanistic interest in ecology, environmentalism and conservation. It influenced the conservation ethics of scientists like Rachel Carson and Aldo Leopold, and the conservation policies of Teddy Roosevelt, all of whom had a nature study childhood.

Of all the educational philosophies discussed in this chapter so far, nature study seems most closely aligned with idea of slow looking as an intentional practice, at least on the surface. This is because the nature study movement straightforwardly encouraged people to spend long whiles looking for themselves at the natural world. Indeed, these prolonged outdoor observational experiences were regarded as the movement's central activity. So it's worth taking a close look to see what the nature study movement can reveal about the promises and puzzles of slow looking as an educational practice.

As Armitage points out, the goals of the nature study movement were very broad—scientific investigation on the one hand, and spiritual betterment on the other—and this breadth meant that different purposes were emphasized by different theorists and practitioners. In 1903, Liberty Hyde Bailey, Chair of the Horticulture department at Cornell University and a major proponent of nature study, wrote: "Nature may be studied with either of two objects: to discover new truth for the purpose of increasing the sum of human knowledge; or to put people in a sympathetic attitude toward nature for the purpose of increasing the joy of living."[12] Bailey leaned toward the latter purpose. He argued that science education, as it is usually practiced, aimed toward making "investigators and specialists."[13] The primary purpose of nature study, on the other hand, is to "to enable every person to live a richer life." This richness has to do with sympathy and connectedness to the natural world. But acquiring it requires rigor. Bailey passionately believed in the power of prolonged, careful observation, and for him, the route to a richer life involved scrupulously seeing nature as it is, rather than over-sentimentalizing it. He approvingly quotes a contemporary of his, the British experimental psychologist E. B. Tichener, who writes about the three dangers in nature-study: "The first is that, in striving for sympathy with nature, we run into sentimentality. The second is that, in avoiding fairy tales, we run into something ten times worse— if indeed fairytales are bad at all; I mean a pseudo-psychology of the lower animals. And the third is that, in trying to be exceedingly simple, we become exceedingly inaccurate."[14]

It is striking that the twin purposes of studying nature that Bailey describes—increased knowledge through close observation, and increased "joy of living" through connection to the natural world—parallel the research findings about students' experience with the Out of Eden Learn program that were described in Chapter 3. You may recall that the program is an online social media-like platform and curriculum that invites students from different parts of the world to explore their own communities and then share their experiences with other students through digital exchange. As part of the program, students take slow walks through their local neighborhoods and document the everyday by writing about, drawing, or photographing things they find striking. Whatever part of the globe students come from, and whether they live in an urban or rural environment or come from an advantaged or less-resourced community, students gravitate toward the natural world. As they walk their neighborhoods, students take pictures of plants and flowers, birds' nests and snake molt; they capture the rough pelt of tree bark and the sleek surface of puddles on the sidewalk. They describe the texture of sand, the multisensory experience of hearing and feeling the wind around them, the soft whirl of cloud formations overhead. When students fill our surveys that ask them to reflect on their experience with the Out of Eden Learn program, these experiences stand out to them. They talk about how fascinating it is to see their everyday environments with fresh eyes and to notice the astounding detail of the world around them. They also talk about the surprising pleasure of slowing down, and how being in nature reminds them of what's important in life. For Out of Eden Learn students, at least, Bailey's two purposes of studying nature—close observation, and the experience of well-being—are synergistic rather than in tension.

Anna Botsford Comstock would likely have been pleased with the union of purposes the Out of Learn students describe, though, like Bailey, she would be careful not to over-sentimentalize it. Comstock, who knew Bailey when she was a student at Cornell and later collaborated with him on designing and implementing a nature study curriculum for the state of New York, is one of the most interesting and important figures in the nature study movement. Comstock was an accomplished artist, naturalist, educator, conservationist, and author of the influential and widely-read book, *The Handbook of Nature-Study*, which has been continuously in print since it was written in 1911. Her work as an educator and a teacher of teachers is especially impressive, and the book is mainly a compilation of essays, lessons, and pamphlets she had written for teachers over the years.

Perhaps even more than Bailey, Comstock links the power of nature study to clear-eyed and careful observation. She opens her book with this definition:

> Nature-study is, despite all discussions and perversions, a study of nature; it consists of simple, truthful observations that may, like beads on a string, finally be threaded upon the understanding and thus held together as a logical and harmonious whole. Therefore, the object of the nature-study teacher should be to cultivate in the children powers of accurate observation and to build up within them understanding.[15]

When Bailey talks about helping children "build up within them understanding," she very much has in mind letting the children themselves do the building. They do this, she believes, by making their own observations, conducting their own investigations, and building their own understandings of the natural world out of what they themselves have perceived. The *Handbook of Nature-Study* is written mainly for elementary school teachers, and it emphasizes this look-for-yourself message strongly. Indeed, Comstock's belief in the irreplaceable value of looking for oneself undergirds her entire pedagogical approach, and she doesn't mince words in telling teachers so: "In general, it is safe to assume that the pupil's lack of interest in nature-study is owing to a fault in the teacher's method. She may be trying to fill the child's mind with facts when she should be leading him to observe these for himself."[16]

Much of the nine-hundred-page *Handbook of Nature-Study* consists in lessons for observing specific plants and animals in students' everyday surroundings. Each lesson presents a single, evocative leading idea through a series of questions that invite students to look closely at something and make numerous observations that build on one another. Comstock repeatedly emphasizes that these lessons should be taken by teachers as suggestive rather than prescriptive, and she is quick to warn that "The direct questioning method, if not employed with discretion, becomes tiresome to both pupil and teacher. If the questions do not inspire the child to investigate, they are useless." Here is the beginning of a lesson involving a hen.[17]

In the 'Observations for Pupils' section, the questions Comstock encourages the teacher to ask may seem simple—perhaps even simplistic. But they are carefully conceived so as to be generative but not overly leading, leaving room for students to observe intently and to and make discoveries on their own. For example, the question "How are the feathers arranged on the breast?" requires students to look closely for themselves

Lesson 1

Feathers as Clothing

LEADING THOUGHT—Feathers grow from the skin of a bird and protect the bird from rain, snow, wind, and cold. Some of the feathers act as cloaks or mackintoshes and others as underclothing.

METHOD—The hen should be at close range for this lesson where the children may observe how and where the different kinds of feathers grow. The pupils should also study separately the form of a feather from the back, from the breast, from the under side of the body, and a pin-feather.

OBSERVATIONS FOR PUPILS—1. How are the feathers arranged on the back of the hen? Are they like shingles on the roof? 2. How does a hen look when standing in the rain? 3. How are the feathers arranged on the breast? 4. Compare a feather from the back and one from the breast and note the difference.

in order to discern subtle patterns. As a comparison, here is an excerpt from a lesson about chickens from another nature study book of the era. Like Comstock's lessons, these lessons are written in the form of questions for students, but in this case the desired student response is given in parentheses.

> How does a chicken fly? (By beating its wings against the air.)
>
> Does a chicken have much flying to do? When does it fly? (To and from its roost)
>
> Do you know what is sometimes done to chickens to keep them from flying over fences? (Their wing feathers on one wing are clipped.)
>
> How does this hinder them from flying so high? (They cannot balance themselves.)[18]

The author may have been a gifted educator in the classroom, but the questions as they are written are very different than Comstock's. Rather than encourage direct observation they seem to encourage students to try to figure out the answer the teacher is looking for, and they have the feel of call-and-response. It may seem picky to harp on these subtle differences of wording. But in school settings where students' entire experience is shaped by how lessons are delivered, the cognitive rewards of slow looking depend greatly on the manner and methods of instruction. It takes a great deal of skill to avoid a rote-response style of teaching in favor of an inquiry-based approach. For all the talk of student-centered teaching at the level of educational theory, teachers tend not to be trained to teach this way, even today in the twenty-first century. The potential benefits of slow looking for students are inextricably linked to the way students are taught. This is a theme that comes up again and again in exploring historical and contemporary slow looking practices—we saw it in the previous chapter about museums—and it is revisited in depth in the final chapter of the book.

The challenge of pedagogy notwithstanding (and it is a challenge not only for nature study but for all the educational approaches described in this chapter), it is interesting to note some of the connecting threads between nature study and the other educational ideas discussed thus far. Like Comenius's *Orbis Pictus*, textbooks on nature study used the everyday objects and experiences of childhood as their starting point. Like Rousseau, Pestalozzi, and Froebel, nature study proponents described their approach as an antidote to modernity, and strove to align their educational principles with what they viewed as natural child development. All of the approaches aim to leverage students' natural inclination to look at things themselves, and they all aim to build on students' direct experience in the world.

The idea of the importance of direct experience brings us to the final educational philosophy reviewed in this chapter—the ideas of John Dewey.

Dewey's Progressive Education

John Dewey was an American philosopher and educational theorist whose ideas have profoundly shaped how we think of progressive education in the twentieth and twenty-first centuries. A prolific writer and active public intellectual, Dewey believed that education offers the most powerful way to shape society for the good. It can do this by developing learners' capacity to think for themselves, so that they can interpret the past in ways that are relevant to their own presents, and so that they can participate thoughtfully in a society that is continually striving towards more just, democratic ends.

Dewey's ideas about learning stand in contrast to a transmissive model of education in which objective cultural knowledge is imparted to passive minds. He believed that students should be invested and engaged in their own learning, and that learning unfolds as a process of "educative experience" which involves a rhythm of doing and undergoing —acting on ideas and materials in the real world, then undergoing the consequences and implications of one's efforts, and then reflecting on cycle-so-far which in turn impels and shapes the next cycle of action. The shorthand phrase for this aspect of Dewey's thought is "learning by doing," and it is associated with a range of educational practices that are familiar to many educators today, most notably problem-based learning, experiential learning, and other constructivst educational approaches in which students have a role in constructing their own knowledge rather than passively receiving it.

On the face of it, there is a clear connection between Dewey's emphasis on interest- or purpose-driven learning and the idea that looking for oneself is a powerful form of learning. In fact, the connection is almost tautological: experiencing the impulse to look at something is a sign of interest; extending the impulse by taking the time to look closely is an act of purpose. Where a puzzle arises is in the connection with Dewey's ideas about the proper goals of prolonged observation and the extent to which they need to be linked to purpose-driven inquiry. This puzzle is worth exploring, because it illuminates some deep questions about the nature of observation. One way to bring it forward is to look at Dewey's changing ideas about nature study.

As a philosopher of education who began his career in the late nineteenth century, Dewey was quite familiar with the nature study movement, which at the turn of the century was one of the major educa-tional movements of its time. Early in his career Dewey warmly embraced the movement; later he came to be quite critical of the way nature study was taught.

In 1894, the 35-year-old John Dewey left his teaching post at the University of Michigan and moved to the newly established University of Chicago. As part of preparing his family for the move, he visited Chicago's Cook County Normal School, which was run by Colonel Francis Parker, a well-known progressive educator. Nature study was at the core of the school's curriculum, and Dewey liked what he saw—so much so that he enrolled his children for the coming year. In a letter to his wife Alice, he wrote: "Every schoolroom there from the first grade up had stuffed birds, squirrels &c; a number had little aquaria; all had collections of rocks &c. the whole school is organized on the 'nature study' principle . . ."[19]

Dewey's ideas about education easily accorded with the twin goals of nature study. Like the nature study proponents, Dewey wanted students to develop the skills of scientific observation so that they could solve real-world problems, but to do so in an integrated, holistic way that would allow them to experience a deep connection to, and community with, the world they were studying. Moreover, Dewey's philosophical views were based in "empirical naturalism"—the view that everything in the world, including all of human activity, can be explained by natural phenomena rather than by supernatural entities or ideal forms, and that human knowledge is developed through experiences in and of nature. As he writes much later in his book *Experience and Nature*:

> Experience is *of* as well as *in* nature. It is not experience which is experienced, but nature—stones, plants, animals, diseases, health, temperature, electricity, and so on. Things interacting in certain ways *are* experience; they are what is experienced. Linked in certain other ways with another natural object—the human organism—they are *how* things are experienced as well. Experience thus reaches down into nature; it has stepped. It also has breadth and to an indefinitely elastic extent. It stretches. That stretch constitutes inference.[20]

Dewey saw the study of nature as a fertile context in which to cultivate students' "educative experiences," and Colonel Parker's school was clearly in his mind as he envisioned his own school, the Laboratory School at the University of Chicago, which he would open a year later. Later on in the same letter to Alice he continues: "There is an image of a school growing up in my mind all the time; a school where some actual & literal constructive activity shall be the center & source of the whole thing, & from which the work should be always growing out in two directions—one the social bearing of that constructive industry, the other the contact with nature which supplies it with its materials."[21]

By 1896, Dewey's school had thirty-two students and was able to hire two full time teachers; one in history and literature, and the other in nature study. Close observation was a central practice of nature study, and Dewey began to worry about how to keep it connected to the natural interests of children. In an 1897 address he gave to parents at the Lab school, one can already hear Dewey's concern:

> To make the child study earth, air or water, bird, beast, or flowers apart from environment and out of relation to their use . . . their function in the total life process, cuts the ties that relates and binds natural facts and forces to people and their activities. The child's interest fades for he misses the way.[22]

Despite these concerns, Dewey of course recognized the importance of close observation in high-level thought, especially scientific thought, and he identified it as a key component in the process of inquiry. Dewey defined inquiry as "the controlled or directed transformation of an indeterminate situation into one that is so determinate in its constituent distinctions and relations as to convert the elements of the original situation into a unified whole."[23] Observation is the first step in the process of inquiry because identifying the observable features of a situation determines "the facts of the case." These observations in turn suggest ideas—i.e., solutions, theories, hypotheses, or possible courses of action—that, as a consequence of being envisioned or enacted, suggest additional or new conditions to observe, which in turn shape new ideas, and so on. As Dewey explains: "Observation of facts and suggested meanings or ideas arise and develop in correspondence with each other."[24]

For Dewey, this progressive cycle of observation and ideation, impelled forward by the goal of solving a problem or reaching a conclusion, is decidedly purpose-driven. As he says in his book *How We Think*, "scientific men never make the accumulation of observations an end in itself, but always a means to a general intellectual conclusion . . ." He goes on to explain that "observation is an *active* process. Observation is exploration, inquiry for the sake of discovering something previously hidden and unknown, this something being needed in order to reach some end, practical or theoretical."[25]

Dewey's concerns about nature study being "isolated and dry" persisted, and by 1916 he critiques the pedagogical practices connected to nature study sternly:

> Everybody knows that nature study has suffered in schools from scrappiness of subject matter, due to dealing with a large number of isolated points. The parts of a flower have been studied, for example, apart from the flower as an organ; the flower apart from the plant; the plant apart from the soil, air, and light in which and through which it lives. The result is an inevitable deadness of topics to which attention is invited, but which are so isolated that they do not feed imagination.[26]

For Dewey, the way to avoid this "deadness of topics" is to make sure that students' observations are driven by their own interests and purposes. Dewey tends to discuss observation in the context of highly purpose-driven scenarios such as problem-solving and hypothesis-testing. But it is worth keeping in mind that the role of purpose in prolonged observation can be considered along a continuum. At one end are situations in which the driving purpose is to solve a central and important problem. An example Dewey himself uses is of a fire alarm in a crowded room.[27] The "problem" is figuring out how to get out of the room; the role of observation is to look around and determine the spatially fixed traits of the situation, such as the location of the aisles and exits, as well as the more fluid traits, such as the behavior of the crowd. Dewey's example is a particularly urgent one, but there are plenty of less urgent everyday examples that cluster towards this side of the continuum, even if they aren't at its extreme end. You might be looking closely at a pile of stones, with the purpose of figuring out how to best fit them into a stone wall, or observing the pattern of birds who visit your outdoor birdfeeder in order to discern which birds are migratory. These are clearly purpose-driven activities, even if they don't have the urgency of fleeing from a fire.

At the same time, there are plenty of examples at the other end of the continuum, where the role of purpose in prolonged observation is more diffuse and fluid. These are experiences in which successive small purposes emerge as part of the unfolding experience of looking, rather than providing its stern backbone. Suppose you are hiking through the mountains and you pause for a while to study a distant vista of a lake ringed by mountain peaks. Your eye lingers on the cerulean blue of the water and then drifts to the mountains above it. You notice what seems to be a hint of a dirt road winding up one of the mountainsides, and you wonder whether there might be a house tucked behind a ridge; your eye follows the slim line of the path to see what you can see. Along the way you notice a barren patch of a hillside with a sparse scattering of saplings. You suspect it may be a site of a recent forest fire, so you look more closely to see if you can discern a swath that indicates the fire's path. These small purposes—looking for a hidden house, or a fire's path—emerge in a way that shapes your meandering gaze. But to characterize the experience as primarily purpose-driven would be to miss something of its texture. This kind of emergent observation is often found in the sciences and arts, and it was touched on in Chapter 2, in the section on the observation of open inventory. There, we looked at how scientists use techniques for making field notes that aim to cast a wide net for observations, even if they presently seem unconnected to a driving research question or purpose. We also looked at the strategies of poets and artists whose goal is to see and capture as much as they can, "everywhere and anywhere." And we looked at the experience of the students in the museum, whose observations followed a freeform path as they built on the observations of their fellow students.

From the standpoint of education, there are risks associated with cultivating students' observational skills at both ends of the continuum. At the strongly purpose-driven end, the risks have to do with the pitfalls of saliency: the more strictly students are trained to look *for* certain kinds of features, the more likely they are to miss important features that are to the side of their attentional focus. The risks at the other end of the spectrum are exactly what Dewey critiques: a mechanical listing of observable features that is detached from students' natural interests and impulses. While Dewey is right to worry about the problem of "isolated and dry" observation, the source of the problem isn't so much the absence of a driving purpose as it is a rigid pedagogy that doesn't make room for students' spontaneously unfolding purposes to shape the flow of their observations.

The solution to this problem is less likely to be found at the level of broad theory than in the subtleties of instructional design and the artistry of teaching. As an example, recall the two contrasting nature study lessons about chickens mentioned earlier. Both were based in the same educational approach—nature study; both were about the same topic—chickens; and both used questions to elicit students' observations. Yet the first one invites students to examine the characteristics of chickens for themselves and to follow the natural flow of their observations, while the second one seems to ask students to rehearse knowledge they already have and to guess at the answer the teacher wants.

This chapter began by making the point that the idea of school is based on the belief that there is value in following an organized pattern of instruction in order to learn effectively. All the thinkers discussed in the chapter—Comenius, Rousseau, Pestalozzi, Froebel, Agassiz, and Dewey—believed that schooling should be organized to bring forward and extend students' innate interest in looking at things for themselves. The thread of this thought plays out differently in their various philosophies, but the overall strand is robust. Still, where the rubber hits the road, so to speak, is in how these ideas translate into practice. As Dewey's critique of nature study shows, it is very easy for instruction that is designed with the best of intentions to slip into didactic lessons in which students' impulse to look at things themselves is cramped and stifled rather than encouraged. We return to this issue in the final chapter of the book and consider how to address it. But by way of the slow road, the next two chapters look first at the connection between slow looking and the history of scientific observation, and then at the different cognitive yields of slow looking—in other words, the different kinds of things slow looking helps us learn.

Notes

1   Comenius, J. A. (1887). *The Orbis Pictus of John Amos Comenius*. Syracuse: C. W. Bardeen.

2   Rousseau, J-J. (1979). *Emile: Or On Education.* (Bloom, A., Trans.) New York: Basic Books. (Original work published 1762), p. 100.
3   Quoted in Armytage, W. H. G. (1952). Friedrich Froebel: A centennial appreciation. *History of Education Journal, 3*(4), 107–113. Retrieved from http://www.jstor.org/stable/3659205.
4   Anonymous. (1874). The Anderson school of natural history. *Nature, 11,* 167–168. Retrieved from http://digicoll.library.wisc.edu/.
5   Ironically, though the Museum of Comparative Zoology is a thriving center for evolutionary studies today, Agassiz was not on the side of history regarding the theory of evolution. A contemporary of Darwin's, Agassiz believed that god had created every species in its current location, and that species did not change over time; rather, they became periodically extinct due to large catastrophes like floods and glaciers. In 1860 Agassiz wrote a review of *Origin of Species* in the *American Journal of Science,* calling Darwin's ideas untrue and a scientific mistake. He opposed Darwin's theories for the rest of his career.
6   Scudder, S. H. (1974). In the laboratory with Agassiz. *Every Saturday, 16,* 369–370.
7   James, W. (1911). *Memories and Studies.* New York: Longmans, Green, and Co.
8   Quoted in Jordan, D. S. (1896). Agassiz at Penikese. *Science Sketches.* Chicago, IL: A. C. McClung & Co., p. 134.
9   Agassiz, L. (1895). *Natural Science News, Vol. 1.* Albion, NY: Frank H. Lattin, p. 186.
10 Armitage, K. C. (2009). The Nature Study Movement: The Forgotten Populizer of America's Conservationist Ethic. Lawrence, KS: University Press of Kansas, p. 4.
11 Ibid., p. 3.
12 Bailey, L. H. (1905). *The Nature Study Idea.* New York: Doubleday, Page & Company, p. 4.
13 Ibid., p. 4.
14 Ibid., p. 139.
15 Comstock, A. B. (1986). Handbook of nature-study. Ithaca, NY: Comstock Publishing Co. (Original work published 1911), p. 1.
16 Ibid., p. 6.
17 Ibid., pp. 30–31.
18 McMurry, L. B., (1913). *The MacMillan Company,* New York, pp. 69–70.
19 Quoted in Hein, G. E. (2012). *Progressive Museum Practice: John Dewey and Democracy.* New York/London: Routledge, p. 23.
20 Ibid., pp. 12–13.
21 Ibid., p. 24.
22 Quoted in Mayhew, K. C., & Edwards, A. C. (1965). *The Dewey School.* New York: Atherton Press. (Original work published 1936).
23 Dewey, J. (1986). The pattern of inquiry. In *Logic: Theory of Inquiry.* The Later Works, Vol. 12. Carbondale, IL: Southern Illinois University Press. (Original work published 1938). p. 104.
24 Ibid., p. 113.
25 Ibid., p. 113.
26 Dewey, J. (1916). Democracy and Education: An Introduction to the Philosophy of Education. New York: Macmillan.
27 Dewey, J. (1986). The Pattern of Inquiry.

CHAPTER 7

Science Learns to Look

In 1551, the physician Lusitanus Amatus published *Centuria I*, the first of what would be seven volumes of medical case histories, each of which contained "100 interesting and instructive cases."[1] A descendant of *Marranos*, the Iberian Jews who had been forced to convert to Christianity but continued to practice Judaism in secret, Amatus was born in Portugal and studied medicine in Spain. But fear of the Inquisition kept him from pursuing his profession on the Iberian Peninsula, and he eventually made his way to Italy, which at the time was enjoying a more tolerant religious atmosphere. Amatus thrived in Italy. He became widely renowned as a physician, teacher, and scholar, and his patients included members of the Italian nobility as well as the Pope. His scholarly lectures, which were accompanied by virtuosic dissections, became famous—he is reputed to have once dissected twelve cadavers in one lecture—and Amatus is credited with discovering the presence of valves in the veins, which led eventually to the discovery of the circulation of blood.

Amatus was an innovator as well as a scholar. When he published the *Centurae*, he arranged the presentation of the text in what was at the time an unusual way: he used a typographical convention that allowed readers to visually distinguish between two kinds of scientific reports. First, in a section presented in standard Roman font and labelled *Curatio*, he described his observations of the features of a medical case. Following that, in a section presented in italics and labelled *Scholia*, he offered his scholarly commentary on the case. In other words, Amatus used textual conventions to make a clear distinction between observation and theory. Moreover, by giving equal treatment to both categories, he shone a spotlight on the rapidly rising status of observation in early modern science.

From our contemporary vantage point, it may seem obvious that making observations is part of what it means to do science, almost by definition: The modern characterization of scientific knowledge is that it is derived from careful, systematic observations, often supplemented by experimentation, which lead to testable understandings of the natural world. But in Europe prior to the sixteenth century, scientific understanding of the natural world was considered to be derived from first principles and general rules, rather than direct observation. Observational knowledge was viewed as having practical value to people like farmers and mariners because it helped with everyday decision-making. But it had the status of lore rather than scientific knowledge. So, for example, observations of weather events might help mariners predict when to sail, but they wouldn't explain the first principles of weather—the general rules which determined weather patterns, nor the first principles from which those general rules could be deduced. The discovery of first principles was a matter of learned scholarly analysis, not direct observation.

It's not that people didn't make and rely on empirical observations before the Renaissance. They did, of course. But as the historian Katherine Park points out, they had only a marginal presence in learned writings. In her essay, *Observation in the Margins, 500–1500*, Park explains that in classical and medieval writings, empirical observations about the natural world were often jotted down anonymously in the margins of texts— usually related to practical concerns such as navigation and farming. Not only was direct perception considered marginal to genuine scientific knowledge, but the term "observation" itself wasn't fixed to a single specific meaning. Pointing to the writings of first century scholar Pliny, whose encyclopedic *Natural History* was widely influential in the middle ages, Park explains that Pliny used the term *observationes* "to refer to both the original process of tracking correlations and the practical rules derived from them, such as the 'observation' that eating an odd number of boiled and grilled snails is particularly good for stomach problems."[2] The double meaning of *observationes* in pre-modern science referred both to the empirical description of something, and to observances, or procedural recipes, related to it.

Amatus's convention of typographically separating case-study observations from speculative commentary was an important move toward sharpening the concept of observation. It also marked what scholar Gianna Pomata describes as an *epistemic genre*—a new convention for writing specifically about scientific observations—that emerged in Europe in the mid-sixteenth century and was quickly embraced by scholars across disciplines. Pomata explains: "In fields ranging from astronomy and astrology to philology and lexicography, from jurisprudence to medicine and to travel writing, scholars wrote new kinds of texts that they presented deliberately, with assertive pride, under the new title of *observationes*."[3]

This new genre foregrounded a concept of observation that sounds familiar to us today. The historian of science Lorraine Daston explains:

> Characteristic of the emergent epistemic genre of the *observationes* was, first, an emphasis on singular events, witnessed firsthand (*autopsia*) by a named author (in contrast to the accumulation of anonymous data over centuries described by Cicero and Pliny . . .); second, a deliberate attempt to separate observation from conjecture (in contrast to the medieval Scholastic connection of observation with the conjectural sciences, such as astrology); and third, the creation of virtual communities of observers dispersed over time and space, who communicated and pooled their observations in letters and publications . . .[4]

This shift in the latter half of the sixteenth century, from observation being at the margins of scientific scholarship to it being a central and celebrated form of scientific activity, was rapid and dramatic. To get a sense of how robust the shift was, jump forward a mere 50 years from the date when Amatus published the first volume of his *Centurae*, and take a look at the print in the following figure.

Made in 1602 by engraver Jan Saenredam, it shows a whale that has washed up on a beach on the North Sea, with all manner of people observing it in all kinds of different ways. Before reading on, you might enjoy taking a moment to look closely at the print for yourself (feel free to use a magnifying glass). What do you notice about the various observational activities occurring in the scene?

The print shows all of society come out to take in a rare sighting. There are several people atop and around the whale, taking various kinds of measurements. Others are touching the whale to ascertain its texture. Shown in the bottom left corner is the artist and his entourage carefully drawing the whale. Standing directly in front of the whale's belly is a nobleman with a feathered hat and fashionable garb. He is probably a duke, and he probably commissioned the print. The handkerchief held to his nose suggests that the whale's strong stench may disturb his highborn sensibilities. Behind the whale, a parade of townspeople as far as the eye can see stream toward the carcass, lining up to get a look for themselves, and perhaps a touch and a whiff as well. From the perspective of slow looking, this is an *event*—with people from all strata of society settling in to do some serious observing.[5] Far from being in the margins, by 1602

Figure 7.1 All of society comes out to observe a whale: *Stranded Whale Near Beverwick.*

Jan Pietersz Saenredam (1601). Reproduced with the permission of the New Bedford Whaling Museum.

the idea that observation was a key way of gaining knowledge had taken hold of the public imagination. Lusitanus Amatus would likely have been pleased.

In the centuries following the publication of Amatus's *Centurae*, much would happen to extend and problematize the activities of scientific observation. Increasingly refined instrumentation would be developed, networks of observers would be increasingly dispersed across time and space and social strata, and ideas about how to achieve observational accuracy would shift and change. But even in the light of these changes, some core features of scientific observational activity have remained relatively stable. They are roughly the same features that Lorrraine Daston described in her characterization of the sixteenth century epistemic genre of *observationes*. One is that observational data isn't anonymous: individual observers or teams or communities of observers are authorially linked to the observations they make, so that observational methods can be scrutinized and observational data can, at least in theory, be reproduced by other observers using the same methods in a similar setting. Another is the separation of observation and theory—the idea that noticing and describing the "whatness" of something involves different cognitive moves than interpreting or explaining what something means. A third is the communication and pooling of observations in a scientific community. This is the idea that others will look at a record of your observations and add, extend, or learn from them. A tacit part of this is the idea that observation reports should be communicated in such a way as to become reliable tools in a community of inquiry. One can imagine that Amatus had this purpose in mind when he published his case study observations in a way that clearly separated them from his scholarly speculations.

Not all observational records serve this public purpose. As we saw in the earlier chapter on description, scientists' early field notes often include informal jottings which intermingle observations, questions, and speculations. But at some point in the arc of scientific inquiry, scientists create observational records with the intention that they serve as resources for other scientists and scholars. These records can take many forms. They might be written descriptions, such as those in Amatus's *Curatio* sections; they might take the form of drawing or diagrams like those being made by the group of artists observing the beached whale. They might be atlases, maps, astronomical models, anatomical drawings, botanical prints, field guides, or any other record that is carefully rendered so as to accurately describe or depict some slice of the observable world in a way that can be studied by others.

One of the main purposes of these observational records is educational: they serve as informational resources for scientists and laypeople. They help train the eye of novice observers—and refresh and recalibrate the eye of experts—by highlighting what to look *for*. Learning to use these records— be they charts, pictures, maps, or field guides—is part of the training of many scientific disciplines, and the records have an aura of objective authority—think a field guide to butterflies, an anatomical chart of the digestive system, or a composite photograph of the phases of the moon.

Like any human rendering, the human-made records of scientific observations can be examined not only in terms of their subject matter, but also for clues about the minds of their makers and the mood of the times. Uncovering these clues is interesting from the standpoint of slow looking, because, like any other form of slow looking, careful scientific observational activity reflects ideas and ideals about how such activity should occur and how its records should be represented—ideas that themselves have a history. The next section takes a closer look at the history of ideas that shape the making and recording of scientific observation. But before reading on, you might find it interesting to explore your own ideas about the topic. I invite you to take a moment to consider the following two questions:

1. What standards or values do you think scientists should keep in mind when they are making scientific observations? In other words, what qualities of mind should scientists strive for in their observational activities?

2. Relatedly, what standards or values do you think scientists should keep in mind when they create records of their observations that are intended to communicate their observations—the maps, charts, prints, and descriptions scientist make available to the wider scientific community?

If you pondered the first question, you might have suggested that the proper qualities of mind for making scientific observations include qualities like being free of bias, being scrupulously accurate, being careful, and being impartial. If you pondered the second question, you may have suggested that the proper standards for creating observational records include being clear, accurate, and faithful to reality; that is, they should show things as they "really are." When you considered either or both questions, the word "objective" may have entered your mind. Which wouldn't be surprising: The idea that scientific observation should aspire to be objective is familiar to us from our twenty-first century vantage point. And although we readily problematize the possibility of *absolute* objectivity, we also intuitively accept it as an aspirational paradigm. More specifically, we may recognize that scientific observations can't help but be subject to some sort of perspectival influence—that is, we acknowledge that there can't really be what the philosopher Thomas Nagel calls "the view from nowhere"— but we nonetheless feel the pull of objectivity as an ideal. But paradigms for making and recording observations have differed over time: the paradigm of objectivity is just one chapter in a longer story.

Historical Paradigms of Observation

In their monumental book, *Objectivity*,[6] historians of science Lorraine Daston and Peter Galison trace the history of three paradigms of observation, which they collectively call "epistemologies of the eye". Each paradigm speaks to the foregoing two questions in a distinctive way. The first paradigm, which they name *truth-to-nature*, is based on the idea that the visual representations of the results of scientific observation—atlases, prints, drawings, maps—should show the essential, archetypal qualities of the observed phenomenon or object. A classic example of this paradigm can be seen in botanical prints and taxidermy, particularly prior to the nineteenth century. These exemplars show idealized versions of species and specimens that highlight perfect versions of their typical characteristics—a perfectly shaped leaf and flower, an archetypical pose of an animal. Even if the specimen is shown in a naturalistic setting—think of Audubon's birds depicted in their natural habitats—the image foregrounds the features the author believes most typify the specimen. Accordingly, the slow and careful observing eye is encouraged to look *for* these regularities and essential qualities in the process of slow looking.

A second paradigm Daston and Galison discuss, termed *mechanical objectivity*, began to emerge in the middle of the nineteenth century. This paradigm emphasizes "objective" record-making that aims to mechanically capture nature as it appears in the moment, in all its imperfections. Originally, photography played a big role in producing these mechanical images, but they could be produced by other means as well. The idea was to follow a strict procedure for recording observation that removed, as much as possible, any trace of human influence. Daston and Galison open their book with a story that beautifully illustrates the paradigm shift from truth-to-nature to mechanical objectivity in the person of a single scientist, the British physicist Arthur Worthington.

Worthington's work focused on fluid dynamics, and he was especially interested in the physics of splashes. His laboratory experiments were designed to help him observe exactly what happened when a drop of mercury or milk hit a hard surface and splashed outwards. He devised elaborate procedures in which a millisecond flash of light would illuminate the drop and allow his eye to register the shape of the splash at the precise moment of impact, which he then drew as faithfully as possible. To be sure, many of his sketches showed slight asymmetries in the scatter of the splash. Worthington knew that some irregularity was inevitable, due in part to chance and in part to the limitations of his powers of direct visual observation. But he assumed that regularity *was* there, and when he selected the drawings to illustrate his findings he chose the drawings that showed the deep symmetry of the ideal splash.

Then, in 1894, he devised a way to use photography to capture an image of the splash, rather than rely on his visual memory. The photographs confirmed many aspects of the drawings he had made, but they showed more irregularities than he had expected. Over time, as his portfolio of photographs accumulated and continued to show asymmetries in each individual splash, Worthington came to an "aha" moment: asymmetry was the *rule* rather than the exception.

By choosing to favor the symmetrical drawings in his scientific publications, he had unwittingly been masking a truth about the ubiquity of variation. Worthington attributed this insight to the fact that he was able to use a mechanical device—in his case, the camera—to remove the

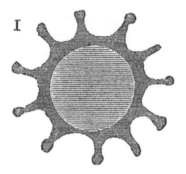 

Figure 7.2 Arthur Mason Worthington, from his studies of liquid splashes. 1876 (left) / 1908 (right).

Public domain.

temptation of thinking he saw what he hoped to see. As Daston and Galison explain,

> Only with those photographs in hand did he come to see that asymmetries and faults were not nearly deviations from some clear and perfect central image—that it was irregularity all the way down. No longer did it make any sense to him to continue to produce the "Auto-Splashes," those idealizations that lay behind, not in, *particular* splashes. He had passed from truth-to-nature to objectivity.[7]

Worthington was a man of his times, and by the late nineteenth century the ideal of mechanical objectivity had taken hold across the sciences. As Daston and Galison are careful to point out, the advent of photography was not the single cause. For one, photographic retouching has been around since the invention of photography—hence, not all photographs are presented as "objective," even from the outset. Also, other procedures can be used to approximate the automaticity of mechanically-made images, such as tracing, or highly supervised handmade drawings. So photography isn't the only machine-like procedure available to scientists. But when used in the service of objectivity, photographs and other mechanically produced observational records could be "free from the inner temptation to theorize, anthropomorphize, beautify, or interpret nature. What the human observer could achieve only by iron self-discipline, the machine effortlessly accomplished . . ."[8]

The ideal of mechanical objectivity dominated scientific observation well into the twentieth century, but it too had limitations. By the second decade of the twentieth century another paradigm of observational activity was emerging. Daston and Galison call it *trained judgment*. It emerged not so much as a replacement for mechanical objectivity, but as an augmentation of it. Machines may be able to produce singularly precise accurate observational records, but they are not able to sort, classify, or discern patterns—although this is on its way to changing.[9] Activities like reading X-rays, classifying stellar spectra, or discerning patterns of brain activity in electroencephalograms required trained judgment in order to "synthesize, highlight, and grasp relationships in ways that weren't reducible to mechanical procedure."[10]

It is not that machine-made records were abandoned. Far from it. But making sense of machine-made records involved more than machine-like procedures. Not incidentally, at the same time that these limitations on mechanical objectivity were being articulated, new ideas were emerging from psychology about the capacities of the unconscious mind. Building on Sigmund Freud's view of the unconscious as a vast churning vat of impulses and desires, psychologists increasingly looked to the workings of the unconscious mind not only as a cauldron of unfiltered impulse, but also as a source of creativity and insight—a place where ideas could be unconsciously incubated, and where huge quantities of information and experiences could be unknowingly sorted and processed, eventually making their way to consciousness in the form of intuitions, insights, and tacit knowledge. This new view of the capacity of the unconscious casts scientists' observational powers in a new light. The "scientific sight" that scientists aimed for under the paradigm of mechanical objectivity depended on suppressing the subjective self. Now, scientists—as well as the expert technicians who assisted them—were seen as having observational powers that were *enhanced* by the subjective workings of the unconscious mind. With their years of experience and training, scientists could look at data and rely on their less-than-conscious discernments to identify patterns, to group and classify data, and discern ranges of normalcy and variation.

This belief, that scientists' intuitive judgment could and should augment machine-generated observations, extended into the computer age. Daston and Galison cite the example of Luis Alvarez, the Nobel prize-winning physicist whose work in particle physics involved photographing millions of particle interactions inside a liquid hydrogen bubble-chamber and devising complex computer systems to help analyze the imagery. Alvarez's radiation laboratory at the University of California in Berkeley was stocked with some of the most sophisticated instrumentation in the world. Yet he insisted that all the people who worked in his lab "were taught to see their scientific images as matters requiring computer-assisted quantification *and* trained judgment."[11] As Alvarez put it in 1966, "More important than [my] negative reaction to the versatile pattern recognition abilities of digital computers is my strong positive feeling that human beings have remarkable inherent scanning abilities. I believe these abilities should be used because they are better than anything that can be built into a computer."[12]

Paradigms Persist

Daston and Galison stress that there is a history to the particular sequence of observational paradigms over time, and that the full flowering of one paradigm emerges to a large extent defined as a reaction to the paradigms of the past: mechanical objectivity emerged as a response to shortcomings of truth-to-nature; trained judgment arose as a corrective to the limitations of mechanical objectivity. But the mindsets of science extend beyond the walls of science strictly defined; they affect the way we think about observation in everyday life, and the emergence of new paradigms doesn't mean that the old ones disappear. All three of these paradigms capture observational moods that are present and familiar to us in everyday experience.

For the mood of truth-to-nature, imagine taking a photo of a striking scene that you want to share with someone else. Maybe it's a picture of an attractive cityscape, or a distant mountain vista. Chances are you'll take several pictures, not just one, varying the angle or height just a little bit each time in an effort to capture the essence of the scene. When it comes to choosing which picture to share, you will likely choose the one that you think best captures this essence, even without being fully aware of the standards that drive your choice.

As an example of the mood of mechanical objectivity, recall the blind contour drawing exercise from the chapter on description. The exercise involved drawing the contours of an object without lifting your hand from the paper and without looking down at the page. Such an exercise reduces the role of judgment and preconception in observation by requiring your hand to trace what you actually see, without checking to see if your drawing represents what you think you see. The mood of the activity is mechanical objectivity: the hand and eye work together as a kind of machine to distance the subjective self from the process of observation.

As an example of trained judgment, consider the seasoned nature guide who takes a group of tourists on a wilderness walk. On the lookout for tourist-worthy sights to point out, she is ambiently alert to all kinds of features in the environment—sounds in the tree canopy, disturbances in the leaf litter, subtle changes in temperature, traces of scents in the air. In response to the group's questions, she might be able to offer an analysis of how to look and listen for salient features amidst this multisensory backdrop. But she herself is following intuition rather than analysis— intuition that has been built up through years of expert experience.

None of the three foregoing scenarios involve formal scientific activities. But they illustrate how the practices and ideals that inform the paradigms of scientific observation also inform less formal observational practices, albeit in a less disciplined and structured way. Still, the practice of slow looking within science is robust, and the history of scientific observation informs our understanding of slow looking simply because science is one of the major arenas in which slow looking takes place.

Scientific observation and slow looking are not the same thing, but they overlap in some important ways. At the foundational level, they share a core epistemological commitment: both are grounded in the belief that careful observation is a key way of gaining knowledge about the world. Also, scientific observation is often (but not always) a form of slow looking, simply because careful and accurate observations frequently take time to make. Further, slow looking, as it has been defined in this book, involves going beyond first impressions, which is often the goal of prolonged scientific observation as well. Slow looking is the broader category, because slow looking occurs not only in science, but across all kinds of domains and disciplines; but it is worth noting that neither looking slowly nor going beyond first impressions are *requirements* of scientific observation: sometimes scientists make observations quite rapidly, either through immediate sense impressions or through instrumentation. And there's no particular requirement in science to go beyond first impressions, so long as scientists' first impressions are based on disciplined, careful observational methods.

Another overlap between science and slow looking is that, like slow looking more broadly, scientific observation is characterized by a cognitive orientation that involves a stepping back from the immersed self. In science, the parameters of this orientation are relatively circumscribed: scientific observers generally aim to make observations that are free from bias and personal interest, and aim for accuracy, clarity, and consistency when reporting their observations. But as we have seen in this chapter, even within these relatively narrow parameters there is room for variation. A truth-to-nature observational orientation seeks essences and regularities; the orientation of mechanical objectivity seeks uniqueness and variation; a trained judgment approach relies on expert intuition to discern patterns and saliences.

When Lusitanus Amatus made the decision in 1551 to separate his medical case study observations from his scholarly speculations by using different typefaces, his innovation was part of a dramatic cultural shift in the way we think about learning through looking. Amatus was a physician and scholar, and his volumes of the *Centurae* were written for a learned audience. But as evidenced by the crowds of people depicted in Jan Saenredam's engraving of a beached whale, the passion for observation extends far beyond the learned class. Some of the people Saenredam depicts are engaged in activities that seem to have a scientific purpose. The men taking measurements or the artists producing a scientific illustration are following observational protocols specific to the time and task, and they are clearly learning something. But many of the spectators seem to be enjoying the pleasures of slow looking in a more general way, by simply lingering and looking, and looking some more. Are they learning, too? And if so, what kinds of insights and understandings might they be acquiring? The next chapter turns to these questions.

Notes

1 The translated subtitle is used by Louis Pelner, in his article, Amatus Lusitanus (1511–1568) a prophetic physician of the 15th century, April 28, 1969, in *JAMA*, *208*(4).

2 Park, K. (2011). Observation in the margins, 500–1500. In Daston, L. & Lunbeck, E. (Eds.), *Histories of Scientific Observation* (15–44). Chicago: The University of Chicago Press.

3 Pomata, G. (2011). Observation rising: birth of an epistemic genre. In Daston, L. & Lunbeck, E. (Eds.), *Histories of Scientific Observation* (45–80). Chicago: The University of Chicago Press.

4 Daston, L. (2011). The Empire of observation. In Daston, L. & Lunbeck, E. (Eds.), *Histories of Scientific Observation* (81–113). Chicago: The University of Chicago Press. p. 81.

5 For a fuller discussion of Saenredam's engraving and its historical significance see Melissa Lo's essay in Dackerman, S. (2011). *Prints and the Pursuit of Knowledge in Early Modern Europe*, Harvard Art Museums/Yale University Press, p. 48.

6 Daston, L. & Galison, P. (2010). *Objectivity*. New York: Zone Books.

7 Ibid., p. 156.

8 Ibid., p. 139.

9 Daston and Galison were writing in 2007. In the intervening decade, there have been huge advances in artificial intelligence, particularly in the development of programs designed to simulate human intuition. In the near future, scientists expect that AI systems will be able to acquire knowledge and extract patterns from data in a process called "machine learning". Machines may indeed be on their way to developing a degree of subjectivity, and to solving human-scale problems. See, for example, Goodfellow, I., Bengio, Y., & Courville, A. (2016). *Deep Learning*. Cambridge: The MIT Press.

10 Ibid, p. 314.

11 Ibid, p. 330.

12 Ibid, p. 330.

CHAPTER 8

Slow Looking and Complexity

All educational philosophies justify themselves by pointing to the kinds of knowledge their workings produce. The justification usually takes the form of a means-end argument: by learning certain things in certain kinds of ways, the argument goes, certain kinds of knowledge or understandings will result. In terms of slow looking, this means that if slow looking is to be taken seriously as an educational practice, one must be able to point to a distinctive kind of knowledge that is evidence of its gains. In other words, whether students are taking the time to look closely at a seashell, a painting, a busy street corner, or the back of their own hand, there should be some demonstrable quality of understanding they acquire.

As the previous chapters have hinted, such a quality does derive from slow looking. When people take the time to look slowly and closely at things, they come to discern multiple ways that things are complex. This is not a radical idea, and several of the education theorists we looked at in the chapter on slow looking and school would likely agree. For example, Friedrich Froebel believed that through sensory exploration of primary forms—cubes, spheres, cylinders—children would come to discern the complex architecture of the physical world. The nature study proponents believed that by looking closely at the natural world, students would come to appreciate the complexity of natural systems, including their own place in those systems.

From an educational standpoint, identifying the discernment of complexity as an outcome of slow looking is useful in a couple of different ways. One is that it can serve as a compass for designing educational experiences that encourage slow looking (design them so that they encourage students to uncover and navigate complexity). Another is that it can help educators know what to look for when they want to assess the outcomes of slow looking (look for signs that students have discerned complexity). But the idea raises as many questions as it answers. For instance, complexity comes in many forms. Consider the human body, which is complex because it is comprised of many physical parts and systems, but also complex because of the many different ideas and customs associated with it. Carefully observing the body will help you appreciate some of its complexities but not all of them. So one question is: What kinds of complexity is slow looking especially good at discerning? Another question has to do with the relationship between complexity and knowledge. Is the discernment of complexity really a kind of knowledge, and if so, what makes it so? Further, even if it is a kind of knowledge, how valuable is it? Not all knowledge is worth the time it takes to acquire, and slow looking definitely takes time. The time/value equation is particularly pressing for school-based educators, who must constantly make decisions about how much time to allot to instruction, and by extension about what kind of knowledge is valuable for their students.

Three Kinds of Complexity

As the example of the human body suggests, things can be complex in different ways. Some kinds of complexity aren't easily recognized through observation, such as the narrative complexity of stories or the conceptual complexity of big ideas like justice or freedom. Nor is causal complexity always easily recognizable. We might be able to see the linear causality of knocking a cup off a table, but not the relational difference in pressure across an airfoil that produces lift.

There are three types of complexity that often make themselves known through slow looking. One is the *complexity of parts and interactions*, which is to do with the physical intricacy or multiple features of things and the way those features interact. Another is the *complexity of perspective*, which is about how things look from different physical and conceptual vantage points. A third is the *complexity of engagement*, which concerns the interplay between the perceiver and the perceived.

These three types of complexity can each be explored individually, and in a moment we will take a close look at each type. But noticing them often twines together in the natural course of observation. A good place to see this in action is in the descriptive work of writers and artists. By way of example, here are three excerpts from a short story by Virginia Woolf, told in the first person, called *The Mark on the Wall*.[1] In the story, an unnamed narrator describes the flow of her thoughts as she sits in an armchair and observes a mark on her living room wall.

She begins with a straightforward description: "The mark was a small round mark, black upon the white wall, about six or seven inches above the mantelpiece."

Even in this simple descriptive sentence, we can hear the narrator going beyond a quick glance to identify the mark's specific features (small, round, black), as well as its relationship to the features of the larger context—the black of the mark against the white wall, and the precise location of the mark above the mantelpiece. By detailing the mark's physical features and location rather than just registering it as a mark and moving on to a new thought, the narrator is beginning to appreciate the complexity of its parts.

The story continues. After dwelling for another moment on the features of the mark, Woolf muses on this early stage of observation. "How readily our thoughts swarm upon a new object," she remarks, "lifting it a little way, as ants carry a blade of straw so feverishly . . ." This reflection pulls her into further ruminations, and for a moment her attention meanders away from the mark. Eventually it returns, but her orientation shifts:

> And if I were to get up at this very moment and ascertain that the mark on the wall is really—what shall we say?—the head of a gigantic old nail, driven in two hundred years ago, which has now, owing to the patient attrition of many generations of housemaids, revealed its head above the coat of paint, and is taking its first view of modern life in the sight of a white-walled fire-lit room, what should I gain? —Knowledge? Matter for further speculation?

Here the narrator plays with the complexity of perspective. Taking first a historical perspective, she sees the mark as "the head of a gigantic old nail, driven in two hundred years ago." Then she takes the perspective of the mark itself, imagining it as an observer of history—perhaps even an observer of her—"taking its first view of modern life."

Finally, after more musings that culminate in a far-flung rumination about archbishops and chancellors, the narrator commits her gaze fully to the mark—and to the present moment—and contemplates her own engagement with it:

> Indeed, now that I have fixed my eyes upon it, I feel that I have grasped a plank in the sea; I feel a satisfying sense of reality which at once turns the two Archbishops and the Lord High Chancellor to the shadows of shades. Here is something definite, something real.

The narrator's sense that she has grasped "something definite, something real" comes about by extending her observation of the mark on the wall beyond a quick glance. In doing so, she naturally touches on each type of complexity—the complexity of parts and interactions, the complexity of perspective, and the complexity of engagement. She just briefly grazes each type, but the example is enough to bring them into relief. Now let's take a closer look.

The Complexity of Parts and Interactions

When we first think of complexity, it is usually the complexity of parts and interactions that come to mind. A car engine; the inside of a pocket watch; a busy restaurant; a pond ecosystem. All of these things have multiple parts, and not all of their parts can be fully observed in a quick glance. Moreover, their parts work together to form a discernible system. The engine parts work together to power the car; the movements of a clock work together to tell the precise time; the cooks and waiters work together to make and serve food; the flora and fauna of the pond area interact to make an ecosystem. Appreciating the many parts of things and how those parts work together is an important kind of understanding. We acquire it when we pursue practical knowledge about how things work; it is a mainstay of scientific knowledge, and we rely on it every day when we navigate the world. Slow looking has a straightforward role to play, because even for the simplest objects and systems, there's almost always more to see than meets the eye at first glance.

Observing the complexity of parts and interactions takes time, and an observation strategy that is well-matched to the challenge is *inventorying*. This strategy, which was discussed in Chapter 2, simply involves taking plenty of time to list all the observable parts of something. In the process of noting parts, many of the interactions between parts also become apparent. Here is a simple example.

On my desk in front of me is an old-fashioned office-grade stapler. I have owned it for as long as I can remember, and I've set myself the task of looking at it closely for a few minutes and listing all the features I see. Here are some of the first things I notice: A metal base and arm. A stainless steel hinged plate directly above the place where staples come out. A beveled edge along the base with a rectangle of plastic fitted into its underside. Several screws on the base and alongside the arm. A worn black plastic cover on the upper portion of the arm, and the word "BOSTICH" imprinted into the metal on the lower portion of the arm. Flaking black paint with brown metal underneath. As I notice these parts, I can also see that many of them interact to fulfill a function. For example,

Figure 8.1
Photo by Shari Tishman.

the arm moves and is attached to the base by a hinge; the stainless steel plate also hinges open to reveal a track where staples can be loaded. The screws connect the sides of the arm to one another and the entire arm to the base. The plastic cover sits on top of the metal arm (I can't see how it is attached) and offers a well-worn press-point for the hand.

Does this little exercise in close looking help me appreciate the complexity of the stapler's parts and interactions? I believe it does: if you had asked me a half hour ago to name the various parts of a stapler and how they interact, it's likely I would have listed far fewer features. Now, if you wanted to press me further and assess the quality of my newly-gained knowledge, you could hand me a stapler and ask me to explain how its parts and interactions are complex. I could probably give you a pretty good answer.

Inventorying is a perfectly adequate everyday strategy for uncovering the complexity of parts and interactions. We use it all the time, even if we don't call it by name, and it worked reasonably well with the stapler. But there are also more precise tools. An example of a strategy that offers a more targeted set of questions comes from the work of Project Zero. Titled *Parts, Purposes, Complexities*, the strategy was inspired by David Perkins' book, *Knowledge as Design*,[2] and in recent years it has become widely used as part of an educational initiative called *Agency by Design—*

a research and development project that focuses on maker-centered learning.[3]

Take a look at the strategy in the box. It asks three direct questions: *What are the parts? What are the purposes of the parts? What are the complexities?* In the context of the Agency by Design project, students in all kinds of settings and at every grade level have used this strategy on a huge variety of objects and systems. To give a few examples: It has been used to look closely at an eggbeater, a tortilla press, a doorknob, a sculpture, a cell phone, a computer, an apple pie, sneakers, chopsticks, a stuffed teddy bear, a toll

Parts, Purposes, Complexities

Looking Closely

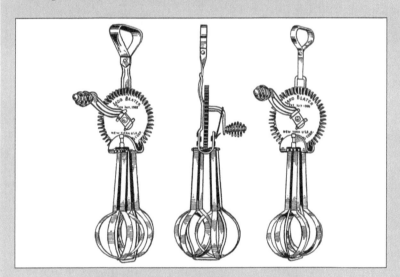

Choose an object or system and ask:

What are its **parts?**

What are its various pieces or components?

What are its **purposes?**

What are the purposes for each of these parts?

What are its **complexities?**

How is it complicated in its parts and purposes, the relationship between the two, or in other ways?

booth, a poem (okay, not exactly a physical object, but still an interesting object of observation). It has been used to examine systems such as a school lunch line, a town recycling program, the process of making an apple pie, the traffic patterns on a busy street, the promotion of a music video, a political protest march, the design of an app. When teachers use this strategy with their students, they often have students work in together in small groups. The students build on each others' ideas, and chart their thinking on a large sheet of paper as they go along. The students' experiences and gains are much like mine with the stapler (though often more profound). They come to appreciate the complexity of parts and interactions by seeing how objects and systems have multiple parts—some of which are hidden or not immediately obvious—and how those parts fit or work together to serve one or more purposes and to create a larger whole.

It is not surprising that the parts, purposes, complexities strategy is particularly popular among educators connected to the Agency by Design project. These are educators who often self-identify as "maker educators", and they specialize in hands-on learning. Some of them run maker spaces or invention studios in their schools; many of them teach some sort of making class—from traditional carpentry classes to architecture to robotics to workshops in soft circuitry. Their fondness for the *Parts, Purposes, Complexities* strategy is noteworthy because one of the criticisms sometimes leveled at close observation as a mode of learning is that it is passive. We saw John Dewey nudge toward this criticism in the earlier chapter on slow looking in school. Dewey worried that instruction that focused too heavily on close observation would feel boring and irrelevant to young people because it asked them to stand outside the action of their own lives—to be onlookers instead of engaged actors. The Agency by Design project, and the research associated with it, makes a very different argument. The premise of the project is that developing a sensitivity to the designed dimension of the world provides a foundation for maker-centered learning, because it allows students to concretely envision the roles and activities of designers, and thus develop a sense of agency regarding design (hence the title of the project, *Agency by Design*). In other words, by learning to see the parts and purposes behind the objects and systems that surround them, students will be more inclined to re-envision, redesign, and reinvent those objects and systems.

The Complexity of Perspective

A second kind of complexity that slow looking can uncover is the complexity of perspective. This has to do with the lenses or stances through which things can be viewed, and it often comes about as a natural consequence of observing the complexity of parts and interactions. For example, consider the stapler again: noticing its many parts, and in particular the company name "BOSTICH" engraved on its arm, naturally led to me thinking about it from the perspective of design. Did the Bostich company invent the stapler? Probably not, but surely someone at Bostich thought carefully about this particular stapler's design, making sure that it was suited to the rugged life of an office tool. Noticing the precise intricacy of the stapler's construction—snug screws, a perfectly-sized slot to hold staples, a smoothly-working hinge—was an easy gateway into wondering about the perspective of the people whose livelihood was connected to its manufacture, such as assemblers and machinists and office workers. How did each of them interact with this object? What kinds of lives did they lead outside of work? Noticing signs of the stapler's use over time—a worn patch on the cover, flaking black paint—was an invitation to wonder about the perspective of the stapler itself. Perhaps in its heyday it led a full and active life in a busy office, stapling hundreds of reports and memos each day. (I can almost hear the clank and bustle of the typewriters and copy machines.) Recalling Virginia Woolf's ruminations about the mark on the wall, I imagine this stapler as a witness to history. Perhaps over time, as its users were enfolded in the digital age and their eyes adjusted to reading onscreen, the stapler was used less frequently. Perhaps the office closed or moved to other quarters, sending the stapler to a storage bin or a secondhand store where it eventually found its way to my desk. (To be honest, I don't know where I got the stapler, though I do know I've had it for many years. Which suggests another perspective: forgetting how things come into one's possession is itself a sobering perspective on the clutter of accumulated stuff.)

Some of these perspectives on the stapler are fanciful; others less so. But all of them bring to mind the web of connections that link us to the objects of daily life. Often these connections are invisible, sometimes imaginary. But they are also what tie us to each other and to the world. Appreciating the complexity of perspective is a way of seeing the stuff and systems of the world in their larger contexts.

A particularly rewarding way to explore the complexity of perspective is through works of art. In Chapter 2 we looked briefly at *The Dove*, a collage by the American artist Romare Beardon. I love this work, and over the years I have enjoyed watching classroom teachers and museum educators explore it with young people. Invariably, the closer and longer students look at *The Dove*, the more they uncover a variety of perspectives that make the work complex. In a moment I'll give some examples of what students say. But first, you might like to revisit the work yourself, on page 18. Begin by simply looking at it slowly for a few minutes. After a while, ask yourself what viewpoints or perspectives might be suggested by or embedded in the work.

When students look at *The Dove*, one of the first things they notice is how most of the identifiable objects in the work—the people, the buildings, the sidewalk and street—are comprised of parts that vary in perspective. The heads and hands of figures are often depicted as large as the rest of the body; windows and doorways jumble together at varying angles; everything is layered so that it's hard to distinguish between surfaces. Students feel the energy of the work first through the perspective of the people in it. They notice the liveliness and busyness of the city street scene—people passing one another, walking, watching, sitting. Eventually they notice the animals; usually first the white silhouette of the cat in the lower-left corner, then the dove atop a ledge, and then the black cat on the sidewalk. Discovering the animals leads students to wonder about the animals' perspectives—especially the dove looking down. What is the dove watching? What is the white cat stalking? Who does the black cat belong to? Often a student will point out that the animals in the collage are shown from a realistic perspective. Unlike the people in the picture, their body parts all look more or less as they do in real life. This leads to a question about the artist's intention: why did he put the animals in as he did? And, because the work is a collage that includes elements of pre-made images taken from other images, some students also wonder whether making the animals look as they do is fully the artist's intention, or whether they looked that way when the artist cut them out (truly an intricate question about the complexity of perspectives).

Often, students have a bit of background knowledge about the work or the artist. For example, their teacher may have told them that the picture is in a museum (it is owned by the Museum of Modern Art in New York), and that it is titled *The Dove*. They wonder about the work as an object of value. How much it is worth? How did it get in the museum? Was the artist rich and famous in his lifetime? Some students might know that Romare Beardon grew up in New York City during the Harlem Renaissance of the 1920s and that he loved jazz. Knowing this—and sometimes even without knowing this—students wonder about how the work would sound if it was set to music, seeing in it a kind of syncopated jazz-like rhythm. They might know that Beardon made the collage in the 1960s during the Civil Rights Movement, which makes them wonder about the meaning of the dove. Very often, students wonder about Beardon's creative process: did he have a full vision of the work before he made it, or did it emerge as he went along? Also very often, students remark on their own familiarity with the scene. Urban students note that they've been in places that feel like this. Students who live outside of cities find it less familiar and wonder what it would be like to live there. Students who live in communities of color or in racially diverse communities often don't mention the skin color of the people depicted in the work. White students who live in predominantly white communities usually mention that the people in the work are Black. Most students notice the cigarettes, and some students view them as artifacts of an earlier age.

In what ways do students discern the complexity of perspective in *The Dove*? First off, they immediately notice the physical complexity of the construction of the collage—its varying layers and angles, and its people composed of perspectivaly different parts. They also notice the contrasting perspective of the people and the animals in the work—both in the way the two are differently depicted, and in the different roles they play in the action of the work. Students also seem to sense complexity in the artist's perspective—wondering about his intentions, and the interplay between his intentions and the process of making the work. Further, in wondering about the work's price tag and museum status, students are exploring the perspective of the work as an object of value and commerce. And finally, students become aware of their own perspective, recognizing that they have a relationship of familiarity or unfamiliarity with the time and place and people in depicted in the picture.

The Complexity of Engagement

The third kind of complexity that is often discerned through slow looking relates directly to this last point, about students' self-awareness as observers. A paradox about slow looking is that because it usually involves a sense of separation between the self and the object being viewed, it's easy to imagine oneself as outside of the picture—to think of one's gaze as detached from the object or scene being observed. But of course it isn't, and the complexity of engagement has to do with probing our own experience as observers. Who are we in relation to what we look at? How do our own ideas and experiences shape what we see? What can we learn about the world by interrogating our own practices of looking?

We have already seen one striking example of the complexity of engagement in the story told in the previous chapter about the scientist Arthur Worthington and his work with the physics of splashes. Worthington was a diligent and careful observer, but it wasn't until he reflected on the assumptions he brought to the act of observation that he was able to see how his beliefs biased what he saw. Because he believed so strongly in the deep structural symmetry of nature, he kept downplaying the asymmetry of the splashes of liquid he was observing with his naked eye. But once he began to use photography, he soon realized that his belief had blinded him to the fact that asymmetry was the rule rather than the exception. Worthington's insight was twofold: he learned something about the physics of splashes; he also learned something about the complexity of looking.

Worthington's droplets were neutral objects: they weren't intentionally designed to get him to reflect on the act of observation, even though they did. But sometimes the object of observation *is* intentionally designed to provoke reflection on the act of looking. Artists often aim for this sort of provocation, and sometimes museum exhibits do, too. A powerful example that brings artist and museum together comes from the work of contemporary American artist Fred Wilson. In a landmark 1992 exhibit at the Maryland Historical Society called *Mining the Museum*, Wilson re-imagined some of the museum's exhibits to bring forward the history of Native and African Americans in Maryland—stories that were largely missing from the museum's exhibits. Wilson critically examined, or "mined" the museum point of view by reassembling the exhibits and bringing new artifacts out of storage. One installation, called *Metalwork*, shows a grouping of gleaming, ornately-worked silver urns and goblets, with a set of iron slave shackles placed in the center. Both the silverware and the shackles are accompanied by standard, neutral-seeming museum labels that give basic information about date and materials.

Figure 8.2 Fred Wilson. *Metalwork 1793–1880.* Installation, 1992.
MTM 010, Courtesy of the Maryland Historical Society.

As soon as viewers take time to parse the exhibit, a benign viewing experience becomes complicated. With the shackles in view, the observer finds it suddenly uncomfortable to look at the silverware simply as fine pieces of craftsmanship, isolated from the context of their production. What else was going on when these silver pieces were made? What sort of society sipped wine from silver goblets and also kept slaves? More broadly, what point of view is reflected in the museum's traditional displays? Whose stories aren't told? And how are we, the museum visitors, complicit in privileging certain stories and histories over others?

In different ways, Wilson's exhibit and Worthington's "aha" moment offer insights into the complexity of engagement by revealing the hidden ways in which our background assumptions shape how we see what is right in front of us. Another kind of complexity of engagement arises when we become aware of our own selves as visible objects—that is, when we see ourselves through others' eyes. A twentieth-century theorist who thought deeply about this was the French philosopher and psychoanalyst Jacques Lacan, who popularized the concept of "the gaze." Lacan originally developed his views as part of a theory of child development: he proposed that very young children experience a "mirror stage" in which they come to realize that they have an external appearance that can be reflected, or "mirrored," back to them in the gaze of others, and this is a seminal moment in the development of self. Lacan later expanded his view and argued that the anxious awareness that comes with seeing oneself as a visible object is an ongoing force in shaping adult identity as well. Lacan's ideas have been influential. In the decades since he originally wrote about the gaze, the concept has been used widely by scholars as a way of exploring the construction of human identity and the power dynamics of human relationships, because it provides a lens for understanding how we define people, including ourselves, through the person or perspective who holds the power of the gaze.

One of the more well-known extensions of Lacan's views comes from the film critic Laura Mulvey. In her 1975 influential essay, *Visual Pleasure and Narrative Cinema*,[4] Mulvey explored how mainstream film is dominated by what she termed the "male gaze". She argues that in most Hollywood films, the film camera puts the viewer into the perspective of a heterosexual man whose gaze frames the woman as a sexual object by looking at her as an object of desire. The viewer—male or female—is often drawn into an experience of slow looking as the camera lingers over the sexualized curves of a woman's body. The gaze creates a power asymmetry: the male gaze actively frames the scene; the woman is the looked-at subject. Thus the male gaze in cinema both reflects and entrenches stereotypical ways of conceptualizing male and female identity. This phenomenon isn't limited to film, of course, nor is it limited to contemporary media. The art critic John Berger made a similar point about the history of European oil painting in his 1972 television series-turned-book, *Ways of Seeing*. "Men act and women appear," he observed. "Men look at women. Women watch themselves being looked at."[5] Discussing the oft-recurring category of nudes in European painting, Berger argued that women are portrayed as having a kind of double identity: "The surveyor of woman in herself is male: the surveyed female," he explains. "Thus she turns herself into an object—and most particularly an object of vision: a sight."[6]

Interrogating the gaze that seeks to define you is one of the most potent ways to explore the complexity of engagement, and it is by no means just the purview of scholars. A powerful contemporary example comes from the 2014 #iftheygunnedmedown Twitter campaign, following the fatal shooting by police of Michael Brown, an unarmed Black teenager in Ferguson, Missouri. The image of Michael Brown posted in the media immediately after the shooting showed a picture that seemed to portray him as menacing. The photo was taken from below eye-level so that he appeared large and looming, and he was making a hand gesture that was perceived by many as a gang sign, though it was actually a peace sign. This image was widely broadcast by the media, rather than another image that was also available that showed Brown looking young and unthreatening. Almost immediately, young people began posting paired photographs of themselves on Twitter under the hashtag #iftheygunned medown, insistently asking: *which would they pick?* One early post shows a picture of a young man wearing a black T-shirt and making a hand sign, paired with another picture of him in a tuxedo holding a saxophone (https://twitter.com/blacksax/status/498637765790019584). Another post shows a youth lounging on a bed and dressed in black, juxtaposed with a picture of him in military uniform reading a picture book to a group of children (twitter.com/IGoBy_Jay/status/498760776019374080). It is impossible to look at these paired images without queasily recognizing how over-ready we are to interpret images according to the stereotypes they seem to reinforce.

The #iftheygunnedmedown activist Twitter campaign arose spontaneously in response to current events. It wasn't explicitly designed as an educational program, but educational programs *can* be intentionally designed to encourage an understanding of complexity of the engagement, and an interesting example comes from quite a different direction: the growing partnerships between art museums and medical schools. Among the outcomes these programs strive for are to encourage medical personnel to question the assumptions and stereotypes they bring to the act of observation, and to recognize how the interpretive stories people construct about works of art—and about patients—can differ despite the same set of data—an outcome the #iftheygunnedmedown Twitter activists would surely appreciate.

A recent forum at the Museum of Modern Art in New York City, entitled *The Art of Examination*, posed a provocative question: can "looking at an Etruscan sarcophagus, a portrait by American painter John Singleton Copley, or an abstract painting by Franz Kline change the way medical students see their patients?"[7] The answer seems to be a resounding "yes". The forum was part of a movement to improve physicians' clinical training by encouraging a more humanistic understanding of health and well-being. The movement is burgeoning: teams of instructors from over sixty medical schools and art museums from across the United States attended the conference to exchange ideas and plan for the future.

The partnership programs between art museums and medical schools are worth looking at a bit more closely, because they serve as a good example of how educational programs can emphasize the appreciation of all three kinds of complexity discussed in this chapter. In their early years, the focus of the programs were mainly on what I would call the complexity of parts and interactions. For example, in 1999, two pioneers in the field, Irwin Braverman, a professor of dermatology at Yale School of Medicine, and Linda Friedlaender, a Senior Curator of Education at Yale Center for British Art, developed a program to enhance students' clinical observation skills.[8] The original idea was to engage students in visual analysis exercises with works of art, thereby increasing their capacity to discern and describe fine details—in paintings, and in the visual diagnosis of dermatological disease. The program was successful, and it served as an inspiration for other programs, such as one at the Frick Museum in New York City, entitled "Learning to Look," in which medical personnel closely examined painted portraits and then applied the same skills to examining photographs of patients' faces.

As similar programs sprang up across the country, their activities expanded: they retained a focus on slow looking and group discussion, but now included activities such as sketching, writing, movement, and meditation. Educators quickly came to see that these programs were doing much more than teaching medical students the technical skills of visual analysis. For example, as participants discussed works of art with one another, they came to appreciate the complexity of perspective by discovering how different members of a medical team might have very different perspectives on difficult topics such as death, privacy, and the role of human touch in medical care. When they looked closely at works of art that had human suffering as their central theme, participants deepened their compassion for sufferers. As they became more skilled in uncovering stories in works of art, they became more attuned to their own patients' stories. Further, these programs were encouraging participants to probe the complexity of their own visual engagement by helping them uncover the biases and preconceptions they brought to the act of looking, and by exposing them to works of art that might disrupt or disturb their tacit ideas about the neutrality of observation—much like Fred Wilson's installations do. Seventeen years after the pioneer program at Yale, the report from the recent forum at MoMA acknowledges this broadening of outcomes. "Many programs have expanded their focus to address empathic communication, compassion, cultural differences, cultural biases and creativity," the report states. These programs "help medical students work in teams, strengthen their observation and communication skills, and develop tolerance with ambiguity and diverse interpretations of information. In turn, these skills are useful in the development of their clinical practices."[9]

Art museum–medical school partnerships are an especially good place to see how the practice of slow looking can cultivate a deep appreciation of complexity. But they are by no means the only place where such learning occurs. Virtually all the stories in this book are offered as illustrations of how it can happen in all kinds of settings and for all kinds of learners: in museums and in laboratories, for kindergarteners and high-schoolers, through the works of artists and writers and inventors and scholars.

At the beginning of this chapter I posed two questions. The first asked whether discerning complexity counts as a kind of knowledge. I hope the examples presented in this chapter have convinced you that it does. The second question asked whether the discernment of complexity is a *valuable* form of knowledge, especially for school-aged youth. This question is especially pertinent for educators. Slow looking takes time, and designing slow looking experiences into a curriculum means making choices to leave other things out. One way to ask the question about value is to pose it in a way my colleague David Perkins did in his book, *Future Wise*[10], which asks: What's *life-worthy* for students to learn? What will help them in the lives they are likely to lead? Translated to our purposes, we can ask: will learning to appreciate the kinds of complexity discussed in this chapter help learners live the lives they are likely to lead? I believe it will. Learning to appreciate the complexity of parts and interactions helps learners understand that the world isn't a black box: they can learn how to disentangle the structural complexity of objects and systems, and in doing so, feel empowered to inquire, tinker, and invent. Learning to appreciate the complexity of perspective allows learners to stretch to see the world from different vantage points, but also encourages them to be sensitive to the fact that we can never truly step inside the experiences of others.

Learning to appreciate the complexity of engagement teaches an important kind of humility: it helps learners understand the role that their own subjectivity plays in their perceptions of the world, and helps them appreciate the integrity of the perspectives of others.

Notes

1   Woolf, V. (1921). The mark on the wall. In *Monday or Tuesday.* New York: Harcourt, Brace and Company, Inc. Retrieved from http://digital.library.upenn. edu/women/woolf/monday/monday-08.html.

2   Perkins, D. (1986). *Knowledge as Design.* New York: Lawrence Erlbaum Associates, Inc.

3   Agency by Design was a research initiative at Project Zero, Harvard Graduate School of Education, with the purpose of investigating the promises, practices, and pedagogies of maker-centered learning. Information and educational resources can be found at http://www.agencybydesign.org/.

4   Mulvey, L. (Autumn 1975). Visual pleasure and narrative cinema. *Screen: Oxford Journals, 16*(3), 6–18.

5   Berger, J. (1973). *Ways of Seeing.* London: BBC Penguin Books, p. 47.

6   Ibid., p. 47.

7   Pitman, B. (2016). The art of examination: Art museum and medical school partnerships. Forum report. MoMA, and The Edith O'Donnell Institute of Art History: The University of Texas at Dallas, p. 11.

8   Dolev, J. C., Friedlaender L. K., & Braverman, I. (2001). Use of fine art to enhance visual diagnostic skills. *Journal of the American Medical Association, 286*(9), 1020–1021. Retrieved from https://www.researchgate.net/publication/11789211_Use_of_ fine_art_to_enhance_visua l_diagnostic_skills.

9   Pitman, B. (2016). The art of examination: Art museum and medical school partnerships, p. 6.

10   Perkins, D. N. (2014). *Futurewise: Educating our Children for a Changing World.* San Francisco: Jossey Bass.

CHAPTER 9

Conclusion: Thinking Through Slow

S low looking is an important and unique way of gaining knowledge about the world. It is important because it helps us to uncover complexities that can't be grasped in a quick glance. It is unique because it involves patterns of thinking that have a different center of gravity than those involved in critical thinking, and different as well than those involved in creativity, though it shares many cognitive capacities with both these areas. Almost anyone at any age can learn to slow down and observe the world more closely, and doing so brings tremendous rewards, both in the knowledge gained and the pleasures offered. But the practice of slow looking takes encouragement, particularly in contexts that may not foreground it as a priority. This chapter sketches three guidelines for creating environments that support slow looking.

Give Looking Time

The single most effective way to cultivate slow looking is to carve out time to let it happen. Obviously this is easier said than done, but one place you might expect to see it happen is in the teaching of subjects like science, in which careful, methodical observation is part of the practice of the discipline. But while extended experiences of close observation might be part of science instruction for older students, these experiences can be surprisingly sparse for younger students. For instance, one study of science instruction in the early years found that observation activities formed just 5 percent of classroom practices for young people, and even those activities mainly foregrounded teachers making observations as students looked on.[1] This finding may be extreme, but it does point to the fact that slow looking often doesn't get cultivated even in contexts where it seems to naturally fit. Another case in point is museums, especially large encyclopedic museums, which rest on the premise that it is worthwhile to behold wondrous objects for oneself, yet often are designed to encourage fast looking rather than slow. Behind both of these examples is a tacit belief that slow looking is part of expert practice—something that mature scientists or sophisticated art connoisseurs do—but not something that is fruitfully practiced by novices. I hope this book has made a persuasive counterargument to this stance: that slow looking is an amplification of the natural human impulse to look at things for oneself, and that the learning accrued through lingering in observation richly rewards the time spent, whether one is a novice or an expert.

In his book *The Intelligent Eye*, David Perkins writes about learning to think by looking at art, and he proposes a set of habits of mind that support both deep looking and deep thinking. First among them is to give looking time. "Persistence and patience are the most important ingredients," he explains, "the commitment to stick it out and see more than you would otherwise see."[2] Perkins makes a distinction between experiential intelligence and reflective intelligence, and he argues that close looking involves both. Experiential intelligence is involved in quick recognition: it helps us make immediate sense of what we see by connecting perception to prior experiences. A child spies a snail on a rock, and, having seen both a snail and a rock before, immediately puts together an impression. Reflective experience is described by Perkins as "the contribution of mindful self-management and strategic deployment of one's intellectual resources to intelligent behavior." Slow looking involves reflective intelligence, because it involves intentionally going beyond a first glance or first impression, and often involves intentional, sustained effort. The child, intrigued by the sighting of a snail on a rock, decides to lean in for a closer look. She may even decide to be systematic in her looking, for example by trying to see how the snail makes its slow way along the rock, or by noticing its different body parts, or by mentally comparing its movements to other creepy crawlies she has observed.

But giving looking time isn't merely a matter of internal mental discipline. The pace and quality of our attentional flow is influenced by the various environments in which we find ourselves. For instance, in museums it is influenced by how galleries are designed, where works are installed, where chairs and benches are located, and how informational text is written. In the classroom, the decision to give looking time often lives with the teacher, who must decide how to build slow looking into the curriculum. Such a decision can be difficult, since giving students time for slow looking usually means giving less time to something else. There isn't an easy solution to this classroom dilemma, but one important piece of the puzzle is for educators to be able to recognize, articulate, and advocate for the learning benefits of slow looking. The foregoing chapter aimed to speak to this challenge by identifying the discernment of complexity as a key learning outcome of slow looking. Sometimes discerning complexity comes about as a natural consequence of letting one's gaze linger. But there is also a strategic side to it, which brings us to the next principle.

Use Strategies, Structures, and Tools to Support Looking

Visual first impressions can be very satisfying. You look, you see, you get it, and you move on. But while it is true that the eye is eager for first impressions, it is also true that we are eager for ongoing stimuli, and offsetting our tendency to stop at first impressions doesn't necessarily require a huge counter-effort. Sometimes all that's needed is a simple bridge to go beyond a mere glance. This bridge can consist of using broad observational strategies of the type we have looked at in earlier chapters, such as making inventories, using categories to guide the eye, adjusting scale and scope, and creating juxtapositions. The bridge can consist of familiar activities like descriptive writing or observational drawing—activities that provide a structure for prolonged observation. Often the bridge is created simply by communicating or recalibrating expectations. One approach, well known to museum educators, is to simply ask viewers: "What more do you see?" Simply by posing this question, the educator communicates the expectation to go beyond a first glance. Similarly, another teaching technique is to structure instructional experiences so that they explicitly require prolonged time for looking. Some extreme examples of this have been mentioned in previous chapters: Jennifer Roberts teaches a course that requires her college students to spend 3 hours in a museum looking at a single painting; the scientist Louis Agassiz insisted that a prospective graduate student spend days looking at a fish skeleton before being admitted to his laboratory. But less extreme instructional designs work well, too. I have often watched educators show younger students an image or object and simply instruct them to take a full thirty seconds to look closely, before talking about what they see. Even this modest slice of dedicated time does wonders to help the eye to slow down.

Another kind of support concerns the availability of props—physical adjustments and tools that support slow looking, such as having a sketchbook or notebook handy; peering through a frame you make with your hands, bending down to view something up close, standing back to take in a broader vista; using binoculars, magnifying glasses, microscopes, telescopes. All of these tools and adjustments calibrate our expectations by offering techniques for going beyond a first glance.

Cultivate the Dispositional Side of Slow Looking

Slow looking is a learningful behavior. It is propelled forward with the aid of strategies and supports like those just discussed, but it also involves more. One way of thinking about this "more" is from the standpoint of character: people who regularly practice slow looking have a certain orientation to learning which is attitudinal as well as skill-based. To put it another way, slow looking is dispositional. This doesn't mean that everyone who is disposed to practice slow looking has the same personality type. Two people can both be close observers but enact slow looking very differently. One person might be stepwise and systematic, another might take an immersive and holistic approach. One person might be curious about the natural world, the other might prefer looking at art or architecture. Still, all of these personality types can be said to share a broad dispositional tendency—the tendency to slow down and take time to look closely. From an educational standpoint, this is important, because conceiving of slow looking as a matter of disposition has implications for how to cultivate it.

Several years ago, a group of colleagues and I were interested in the idea of "thinking dispositions"—intellectual patterns of behavior like careful reasoning, thoughtful decision making, and intellectual open-mindedness. At the time—this was in the mid 1990s—there was a lot of talk in educational circles about the importance of teaching critical thinking skills, and many educational programs were developed that promised to teach them. But by and large these programs didn't transfer very well between disciplines. For example, students might learn how to reason with evidence in science class, but then fail to weigh evidence appropriately in history class or to apply their evidential reasoning skills to issues outside of school. What would it take, my colleagues and I wondered, to cultivate critical habits of mind with a wide reach? Eventually we proposed a possible answer, which took the form of an explanatory framework. At the time, we were mainly concerned with dispositions related to critical thinking, but the framework applies to almost any kind of broad dispositional tendency, including slow looking. It states that there are three interrelated components of dispositional behavior, and that all three need to be present in order for dispositional tendencies with the strength to cross contexts to take hold.

The first component is *ability*. This refers to the obvious fact that in order to engage in any sort of intellectual behavior, it is essential to have the basic capacity to do so. In terms of slow looking this might mean having the capacity to discern visual details, along with the ability to use broad observational strategies like making lists of features or using categories to identify different kinds of features. Possessing some basic ability in these areas doesn't mean one needs to be an expert—just that one can enact the basic moves.

A second component of dispositional behavior is *inclination*. This refers to the motivational dimension of behavior and points to the fact that there has to be some felt impetus for dispositional behavior to occur. In other words, not only do you have to be *able* to do something, you have to want to do it, too. This may seem obvious, but actually people often possess skills they aren't motivated to use regularly. As a personal example, I have the basic ability to keep my computer files organized. Sadly, I sometimes lack the motivation to do so, and few people who know me would accuse me of the disposition to be organized.

The third necessary dispositional component is termed *sensitivity*. This component isn't quite as obvious as the other two. It points to the fact that in addition to having skills and inclination related to a particular disposition, you also have to notice, or be sensitive to, occasions when it makes sense to enact the behavior. To continue with the example of my computer files: As I mentioned, I have the basic ability to be more organized than I am. And although I often lack the inclination to do much about it, I do occasionally feel a flare of motivation, especially when I suffer the frustration of not being able to find an important document. My problem, though, is that as I am busily working away at my computer, I fail to notice moments when small acts of organization would be really helpful. How does this apply to slow looking? Think back to the students in the Out of Eden Learn program that we learned about in Chapter 3. Recall their enthusiasm for taking slow walks in their neighborhoods and seeing their everyday surroundings with fresh eyes. The students' comments and photographs clearly show that they have some basic ability with regard to slow looking, and also that they feel motivated to engage in it. What we don't know is whether their newfound enthusiasm will extend to new contexts, so that they engage in slow looking in other situations where there may not be a curriculum that explicitly cues them to do so— at the museum, for example, or in science class, or simply walking home from school.

The idea that dispositional behavior depends on the coalescence of these three components—ability, inclination, and sensitivity—may sound good in theory, but in the mid-1990s when we proposed the framework, that's all it was: a theory. So we decided to put it to the test. We devised a sequence of written activities for middle school students that allowed us to see whether these three elements were actually present, and separable, in students' intellectual behavior. We discovered that indeed they were.[3] For example, we found some students who had all three elements in abundance; they were able to think critically in situations where it was appropriate to do so, even when the thinking in question wasn't explicitly cued. Some students were motivated to think in certain ways but didn't recognize occasions to do so (like me and my computer files). Some students possessed certain thinking skills but lacked the motivation to use them. And so on through the various combinations. Naturally, once we were able to identify the contribution of each of the three elements to students' intellectual behavior, we were eager to identify the most common shortfalls. What were students missing most often—ability, inclination, or sensitivity? (We had tentatively predicted it would be motivation.) The finding was somewhat surprising.

It turns out that when students lack certain thinking dispositions, much of the time it's not because they don't have the right thinking skills, nor is it because they don't have the inclination. Rather, it's because they don't have the sensitivity to occasion. In other words, people often don't think critically or creatively simply because they don't notice times when it makes sense to do so. This may sound odd, but if you think about it, it's actually not, because formal instruction often acts as a substitute for sensitivity, particularly in the context of school. A lesson designed to teach a certain kind of thinking—careful reasoning, say, or slow looking—*cues* students as to what kind of thinking is called for, simply by virtue of its presence in the curriculum: students don't need to develop sensitivity to occasion, because the occasion is already recognized for them.

How does this analysis of dispositional behavior relate to slow looking? It suggests that in order to cultivate slow looking as an enduring expression of character rather than as a mere deployment of skill, it's important to attend to all three elements of the dispositional triad. Developing ability involves learning to use the kinds of strategies discussed in the foregoing section— strategies and structures for seeing more, for focusing the attention, and for seeing in new ways. Developing an inclination toward slow looking involves accessing the natural human impulse to look for oneself, and extending that impulse by "giving looking time" so that the intrinsic pleasure of discovery has a chance to unfold. It also involves finding or creating environments that support and reward slow looking. Which connects to the third dispositional element—sensitivity. Developing an abiding alertness to occasions to engage in slow looking—an alertness that transfers across disciplinary and contextual boundaries—is a special challenge, particularly in the structured environment of school, which functions as a kind of a substitute for sensitivity by telling students what to do and when to do it. There is no magic recipe, but from the standpoint of educational design, a large part of the answer is to make slow looking a pervasive and enduring part of the cultural surround, instead of a one-off experience or lesson.

Educator Ron Ritchhart and others have written about the cultural forces in the classroom that shape the development of students' thinking dispositions.[4] They are present in the day-to-day life of the classroom, and they exert themselves through the kinds of thinking are modelled, assessed, and visibly valued. So, for example, if you are a teacher and you want your students to develop a tendency toward slow looking, you'll want to make sure that you show students exemplars of slow looking in action by modelling it yourself, and pointing to it in others. You'll want to make sure to make time for slow looking and give it prominence across the curriculum. You'll want to offer students informative feedback that validates their efforts and makes their successes salient. You'll want to make the processes and tools of slow looking pervasively visible in the classroom—for instance by writing down students' observations and keeping them visibly present, and by creating visually enticing classroom displays of observable objects, accompanied by comfortable seating and tools such as magnifying glasses that invite observers to linger.

You'll also want to make sure that there are frequent occasions to make looking social. Each of us has our own set of eyes, so it is easy to default to the idea that close observation is an individual activity. But it can also be powerfully social. Remember the school group that was discussing Shaw's Memorial at the National Gallery of Art, described in an earlier chapter? As the group talked about the sculpture, one student's observations would spark someone else to see something new, which in turn would spark someone else. Together, their collective observations were much richer and more plentiful than they would have been if each student looked silently and solo. The same was true for the adult medical professionals described in the previous chapter, who shared observational experiences in museums.

Looking and Thinking

For most of my professional life I have been an educational researcher. My work focuses on what is often called "high-level thinking", which can loosely be described as the cognitive processes involved in critical, reflective, and creative thought. I believe in an active, hands-on and minds-on approach to learning, in which learners are actively involved in thinking for themselves and constructing their own ideas. Given this background, my interest in slow looking might seem odd. Slow looking can often appear passive—at least on the outside—because it is about collecting observations rather than actively forming interpretations and solving problems. There are many places in this book where I seem to talk about slow looking as an active form of thinking. But is it really? Indeed, is it even thinking at all?

There is a low-bar and high-bar way to answer the question of whether slow looking is a form of thinking. The low-bar way defines thinking as any conscious mental activity. Given this definition, to the extent that we are conscious of the observations we make when we look at something, slow looking easily qualifies. The high-bar way characterizes thinking as an active, engaged experience, in which the mind "acts" by doing things with and to the mental stimuli that flow to it—for example, by examining, analyzing, interpreting, considering, wondering, envisioning, probing, discerning. This is usually the kind of thinking educators have in mind when they talk about teaching students to think. I believe that much of the time, slow looking meets this high bar as well.

Imagine a continuum of high-level thinking activities, with *deciding* at one end of the continuum, and *discerning* at the other end.

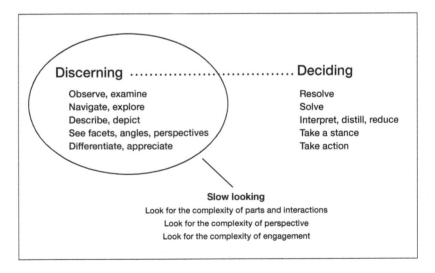

Figure 9.1 A continuum of thinking-centered learning outcomes.

The activities that cluster toward the deciding end of the continuum have to do with figuring out what things mean or what's correct or what to do. They include the types of cognitive activities typically associated with critical thinking: weighing evidence, forming interpretations, constructing arguments, developing opinions, solving problems, and taking considered action. The activities that cluster toward the discerning end of the continuum are those that have been described throughout these pages. They involve creating descriptions and depictions, making prolonged observations, noticing parts and relationships, looking from various vantage points, and seeing with fresh eyes. In education circles, most discussions about high-level thinking tend to gravitate toward the "deciding" end of the continuum. They focus on either critical thinking, which is standardly defined as "reasonable, reflective thinking that is focused on deciding what to believe or do,"[5] or creative thinking, which has to do with seeing beyond the obvious, usually in order to solve problems in innovative ways. Though slow looking can play a very useful role in both critical thinking and creative thinking, subsuming it under either of these headings fails to do justice to its unique processes and goals. Slow looking is *not* primarily judgment oriented, though its fruits certainly inform good judgements. Rather, slow looking emphasizes deferring judgment in favor of apprehending the complexity of how things are at the moment. Nor is slow looking solution-oriented, though, as with making judgments, the fruits of slow looking can certainly contribute to solving problems. Rather, instead of emphasizing change or improvement, slow looking emphasizes describing or depicting the "whatness" of things as they are.

Of course, critical thinking, creative thinking, and slow looking are not three entirely separate realms of cognitive activity. They all depend on one another and often blend together in practice. Moreover, the lists of cognitive capacities associated with each one are not mutually exclusive. For example, seeing things from different vantage points is important in all three modes of thought; sorting and analyzing visual clues can be important in all three areas as well, as can forming evidence-based explanations of how things work. But each of the three areas has a distinct center of gravity. It is useful to understand how these centers of gravity differ, and to understand how the practices of slow looking gravitate toward the "discerning" end of the continuum of thinking-centered learning outcomes. These understandings can inform the design of slow looking experiences, and they can also help educators explain and justify the value of slow looking to others—including students, parents, school administrators, and anyone else who has a stake in student learning.

I hope this book has convinced you that there is more to slow looking than simply slowing down in a fast-paced world. Slow looking is an important mode of learning. It plays a role in science, art, and everyday life, and it can fruitfully be practiced by almost everyone—experts and novices, young people and adults. Above all, the value of slow looking lies in doing it for oneself. No amount of outside information or second-hand reports can replace either the insights it yields or the pleasure it provides.

Most of the educators I know, whether they teach preschoolers or graduate students, care about empowering their students to understand the world around them, and to live within it with intelligence and compassion. As a practice, slow looking has a lot to offer. It helps us uncover the intricacies of objects, systems, and relationships. It allows us to envision and explore diverse perspectives while at the same time probing our own subjectivity. And it helps us discern and appreciate complexity without necessarily dissolving it. The value of slow looking can be summed up in a phrase: The more we look, the more we see.

Notes

1   Kallery, M. & Psillos, D. (2002). What happens in the early years science classroom? The reality of teachers' curriculum implementation activities. *European Early Childhood Education Research Journal*, 10(2): 49–61.

2   Perkins, D. N. (1994). *The Intelligent Eye*. Santa Monica, CA: The Getty Center for Education in the Arts, p. 36.

3   Perkins, D., Tishman, S., Ritchhart, R., Donis, K. & Andrade, A. (2000). Intelligence in the wild: A dispositional view of intellectual traits. *Educational Psychology Review*, 12(3): 269–293. For a more practitioner-oriented discussion, see Tishman, S. (2001). Added value: A dispositional perspective on thinking. In A. Costa (Ed.), *Developing Minds: A Resource Book for Teaching Thinking*. Association for Supervision and Curriculum Development (ASCD), revised edition, vol. 3, 72–75.

4   See Ritchhart, R. (2015). Creating Cultures of Thinking: The 8 Forces We Must Master to Truly Transform Our Schools. San Francisco: Jossey-Bass; and Tishman, S., Perkins, D., & Jay, E. (1995). The Thinking Classroom: Teaching and Learning in a Culture of Thinking. Needham, MA: Allyn & Bacon.

5   Norris, S. P., & Ennis, R. H. (1989). *Evaluating Critical Thinking*. Pacific Grove, CA: Critical Thinking Press, p. 3.

Index

 Taylor & Francis eBooks

Helping you to choose the right eBooks for your Library

Add Routledge titles to your library's digital collection today. Taylor and Francis ebooks contains over 50,000 titles in the Humanities, Social Sciences, Behavioural Sciences, Built Environment and Law.

Choose from a range of subject packages or create your own!

Benefits for you

» Free MARC records
» COUNTER-compliant usage statistics
» Flexible purchase and pricing options
» All titles DRM-free.

Benefits for your user

» Off-site, anytime access via Athens or referring URL
» Print or copy pages or chapters
» Full content search
» Bookmark, highlight and annotate text
» Access to thousands of pages of quality research at the click of a button.

REQUEST YOUR **FREE** INSTITUTIONAL TRIAL TODAY	**Free Trials Available** We offer free trials to qualifying academic, corporate and government customers.

eCollections – Choose from over 30 subject eCollections, including:

Archaeology	Language Learning
Architecture	Law
Asian Studies	Literature
Business & Management	Media & Communication
Classical Studies	Middle East Studies
Construction	Music
Creative & Media Arts	Philosophy
Criminology & Criminal Justice	Planning
Economics	Politics
Education	Psychology & Mental Health
Energy	Religion
Engineering	Security
English Language & Linguistics	Social Work
Environment & Sustainability	Sociology
Geography	Sport
Health Studies	Theatre & Performance
History	Tourism, Hospitality & Events

For more information, pricing enquiries or to order a free trial, please contact your local sales team:
www.tandfebooks.com/page/sales

 Routledge
Taylor & Francis Group

The home of
Routledge books

www.tandfebooks.com